*in general and prison ministry in particular... It may also
challenge a lot of perceptions both about prisoners and also
about clergy."*

The Venerable Michael Kavanagh. Head of Prison
ervice

524 772 42 4

JAIL BIRD

The inside story of the Glam Vicar

SHARON GRENHAM-THOMPSON

LION

Published by Lion Books
an imprint of
Lion Hudson plc
Wilkinson House, Jordan Hill Road,
Oxford OX2 8DR, England
www.lionhudson.com/lion

ISBN 978 0 7459 6877 3
e-ISBN 978 0 7459 6878 0

First edition 2016

A catalogue record for this book is available from the British Library

Printed and bound in the UK, June 2016, LH26

*For reasons of security and sensitivity most names have been changed, as well as some very minor
details. However, all events and people are real, and described as I remember them.*

To Dad

CONTENTS

FOREWORD

By Chris Evans

I have worked with Sharon, the Glam Vicar, for five years, since right from the beginning of my tenure on the Radio 2 *Breakfast Show*.

"How do you feel about *Pause for Thought?*" I was asked when preparing to take over from the late great Sir Terry Wogan. The powers that be were nervous I would request that the daily dose of sober and insightful contemplation be quietly sidelined elsewhere.

"I love it," I declared instantly, which was and remains the absolute truth. Just as I love *Prayer for the Day* and *Thought for the Day* on Radio 4.

Whether you are religious or not, these "moments", when done well, speak to us more as humans than believers or followers. This is why I encourage our contributors to lead with everyday philosophy, reflection, and common sense first before anything else.

Simply declaring "God" says this and "God" says that is a real Marmite approach, preaching usually only to the already converted, those already on the bus. Whereas common-sense lessons drawn from historical scriptures and parables are much more colourful, communicable, believable, and entertaining.

Sharon gets this totally. She always has. She is also a brilliant writer, as you are about to find out.

What follows on the pages of this book crystallized for me how come she connects so directly with people. The ability to connect is all about "the well". The well of emotions and experiences we each have to draw from. The thing is, I had no idea Sharon's was so deep.

But of course I should have known. Over the years during our many and varied "on air" exchanges, I have "felt" more than she's told me, "observed" more than perhaps she might have wanted to let on and often "heard" more in between the lines as she takes a breath before reading on, than from the lines themselves.

But let me tell you, all that changed when I turned the first page. Chapter after chapter, this book is surprising, funny, enlightening, reassuring but, above all, brutally and breathtakingly honest. Totally gripping and extremely personal, this fluid autobiography comes gushing down the mountain like a raging floodwater. I literally couldn't put it down. In fact I read the whole thing in one session.

We are all of us fragile and fallible and there's nothing wrong with that. On the contrary, it is only the fragile and fallible who know what it is like to be truly strong. Strength without suffering and vulnerability is merely good fortune unfettered by any palpable reality. Easy Street by comparison.

To fully appreciate life, you have to have washed the stench of death from your clothes. Or felt the cold and rain of loneliness day after day, all the way through your skin and into your bones. Or had nights of quaking misery through no fault of your own that left you cowering in bed, holding yourself so tight sleep was an impossibility.

This is a very special female vicar's account of her exposure to such things. Much of what's bad in life that she has somehow converted into a formidable force for good.

Dear Lord,
We need more like this one please.
Amen.

INTRODUCTION

He who would valiant be, 'gainst all disaster,
Let him in constancy follow the Master.
There's no discouragement shall make him once relent
His first avowed intent:
To be a pilgrim.
(John Bunyan)

The sound of the organ filtered through to us as we stood in the breezy cloister. The unfamiliar weight of the robes lay across my shoulders, as if to remind me of the promises that lay beyond the heavy wooden doors. I tugged once again at the stifling dog collar close about my neck – usually I went for something a little lower cut. I smiled at Martin, a fellow "baby vicar", standing next to me. "Can you believe it?" I whispered. "We made it."

And then there was a shushing and a shuffling, and we were off – briefly out into the sunlit quad of Christ Church, Oxford, before stepping through those doors to a sea of faces and beautiful treble voices singing… the theme tune from *The Vicar of Dibley*.

If I had the proverbial pound for every Dibley reference I've parried since the day of my ordination in 1998, I'd at least manage a decent night out in London. But it was still early days for women in the Church of England then, and media representations of "lady vicars" were few and far between. Dawn French's wonderfully bonkers village priest was, for many years, the only image of an ordained woman reaching the mass market.

It's very different now of course, and Twitter's awash with my female colleagues, not to mention the women priests who are TV faces, fashionistas, and leading lights for social change. Bishops, too! Given that a good few years have gone by since I was ordained, I'm now one of the older generation of female priests – but amongst the many things I'm thankful for, one is that I managed to nab the epithet "Glamvicar" before anyone else did.

Whether it's on social media, in print, on the airwaves, or even in the flesh, I do my best to live up to the tag. I've been amazed at the opportunities that have come my way: I've dined with aristocrats, hugged Harry Potter (well, Daniel Radcliffe…), and joked with an archbishop. I love presenting live on radio, and it's still childishly exciting when someone in an obscure bed and breakfast in Wales says to me, "Oh you're that double-barrelled vicar woman from Radio 2! I love listening to you!" I'm sure there are equal numbers who groan and switch me off – I've done it plenty of times to others myself. But it's fun, I try not to take it all too seriously, and – given the capricious nature of the "meed-ya" – I know it won't last for ever.

What *does* last for ever, or at least a very long time, is the legacy each of us leaves behind. I went into the church because I believed (and still do) that I had something constructive to offer the world. I'm hugely grateful that I'm allowed a pulpit to millions via radio every now and then. But I'm also acutely aware that what I do day to day has to count even more.

And I have to say, the day job is pretty unglamorous.

Having qualified as a solicitor after university, when I then came to be ordained, several of my friends nodded sagely and predicted I'd be a prison chaplain one day. "No way," I retorted. "That's not me at all."

Ha blooming ha. Nearly two decades on, I'm amazed to find I've been inside for nearly half of that time. These days I'm the Senior Chaplain at HMP Bedford, a male category B prison (which means it's not the very highest level of security, but it's the next rung down, housing some pretty serious offenders). I also have a couple of other jails under my (chain-festooned) belt. It's a strange job for a woman – but OK, I give in – I love it. Most days. And I'm clearly living proof that God has a sense of humour.

I never intended or expected to take this path in life – and some of the coincidences make me laugh out loud. But as I've established my accidental career (or "ministry" as church-speak would have it – career's a bit of a dirty word), I've been able to tie together so many threads in my own life, as well as gain an insight into the struggles and sorrows of people not really so very different from the rest of us, despite the distance we might like to create between ourselves and offenders in jail.

This isn't a book about theology, or politics. I'm not learned, and I don't have answers, but I do have my reflections, pieced together from my own long and winding road. I've seen and heard things I wouldn't wish on anyone, come home some nights stunned and exhausted, and wept at times out of sheer frustration at the system. But I've stayed, even when other, more glamorous, sirens have been calling. It seems crazy to say it, but I've always been someone who didn't quite fit, and in jail, ironically, I seem finally to have found where I belong.

I wrote this book in the Autumn of 2015. I had no idea that by the time it was published I would no longer be a prison chaplain. But while life can change, I believe the stories I share in these pages remain as relevant as ever.

TO BE A PILGRIM

It was a sunny March day in the late 1970s. As the car pulled up on the gravel drive, I looked out of the window at the grand building filling the view. It was made of pale stone, set against a clear blue sky, with a semicircular stone staircase leading up to a set of double doors. To the right was a terrace, covered in ivy, with a gate leading through to another terrace, and then extensive playing fields, tennis courts, and a long avenue of lime trees. To the left were more buildings – huge, brown brick, with long vertical windows suggesting an enormous hall above the first floor level, and smaller, arched windows at ground level, looking a bit like the nether regions of a London station.

There were cars everywhere (a lot posher than ours, I noted immediately) and a stream of girls, all ages and sizes, but all dressed in the odd combination of brown and blue that eventually became my much-loathed attire for the next half decade. This was the North London Collegiate School for Girls, and I was about to take the entrance exam.

My family had only flown in from Gibraltar a couple of weeks previously. We'd been posted there since July the year before, and I'd been an army brat. Now my stepfather had changed his post, bringing us back to the UK. I was still missing the friends I'd begun to establish on the Rock, and pretty fed up about having to move *again*. Since Mum and Dad split up three years ago, and then Mum remarried, it felt like we'd been constantly on the move.

I'd already sat one entrance exam for a different school, and passed easily. Today would give me a comparator. It was certainly bigger; and as the gracious, but to my eyes somewhat intimidating, deputy headmistress took us on a tour, I could see that the facilities were amazing. Good old Dad – I hadn't really known much about the financial wrangling connected to the divorce, but I did know the upshot was that Dad paid school fees. We weren't a wealthy or well-connected family by any stretch of the imagination – but my mother's aspirations, Dad's hard work, and my rather surprising intellectual sharpness proved to be a pretty lucky combination.

I passed the Maths, English, and French papers, and the interview, despite being pulled up for not being able to spell "separately" (that one still makes me anxious). A couple of weeks later, at the start of the summer term, I joined the brown-and-blue clad young ladies and once again began the task of fitting in and finding out.

I'm not sure whether I distinguished myself or blotted my copybook on that first day – probably both, depending on whether the onlooker was a teacher or a classmate. Having been brought to class after morning registration, introduced to the thirty or so faces that greeted me as a new girl, and then left to it, I started off confidently enough.

"Have you just moved?"

"Where are you from?"

"Why are you starting late?"

I parried the barrage of questions, my recent provenance from the Med being deemed interesting enough to earn me the offer of sweets, a flurry of introductions, and a promise to show me round at break-time. It was the next question that my already highly attuned social radar twitched at.

"What does your father do?"

"Oh," I replied airily, aware that this could make or break me in what was quite obviously a privileged circle and deciding not to explain the stepfather thing, "he used to be in the army, but since we moved he's going into business or something." And with that I turned the questions around, asking about the form teacher, the rules, anything I could think of to deflect the attention away, however kindly meant. Although as an adult I was later to learn just how varied and far from privileged many of my contemporaries were, it was still a long time before I confessed to any of my peers the complications and confusions of my family life.

The morning came and went, lunch in a vast dining hall – the place with the railway arch windows – and back to classroom Upper Three Thirteen, to await the afternoon's lessons. Rosie had a tennis ball, and three of us began a game of catch around the room, standing on the wooden-lidded desks and bouncing the ball off the desks in between. Several others gathered, and soon we were all laughing, and I felt as if I'd been there months, not hours. Buoyed up, I gave the ball a bit of a flourish as I threw it.

Bad idea. I don't think I've ever bowled a spin ball since, but I certainly did that day. Narrowly missing Rosie, it hit the corner of a desk, careened upwards, and hit the ceramic lightshade hanging in the centre of the room. Shattering it into a thousand glittering pieces. On. My. First. Day.

With impeccable timing, the form teacher bustled through the door, and as she hit the stunned silence, she visibly recoiled.

I looked at Rosie. Who gaped at me. Alison, Sarah, Jane – all their eyes were wide; you could practically see the panicked thoughts racing across their minds.

"What do you think you are doing?" Mrs L.'s voice unfroze the scene.

"I'm sorry," I whispered. "It was me; it was an accident."

Dispatched to find a dustpan and brush, I was saved by my status of "new girl", and into the bargain somehow seemed to have passed an initiation test with my classmates. I would spend most of the next six years with them, and in some ways they became the family I would often feel I lacked. My best friend was one of those classmates, and she and I have grown up and grown older together, our kids more like cousins than just buddies. Thanks to reunions and Facebook, several of us have stayed in sporadic touch. We've seen tragedies and success, love and loss, but put us together and we're giggling teenagers again.

I wasn't a classic naughty girl at school, but it's probably true to say my independent, free-spirited streak got me into trouble on more than one occasion. I would meet local boys at the bottom of the vast playing fields, which were out of bounds, traipsing across the local park at lunchtime with my friend to try out cigarettes, and flout the school uniform rules as often as I could. It wasn't much of a teenage rebellion – I was always too terrified of being found out and parents being summoned – but I lived with tight controls at home, and high expectations at school. The steam had to escape somewhere. In fact, it wasn't really until my university years that things threatened to get out of hand – so for now I pushed the boundaries just far enough to get away with it, and thrived in the creative swirl of possibilities presented to me in my protected suburban world.

The headmistress at the time was nowhere near as scary in manner as her deputy, but she was the kind of lady (and I use that word advisedly) whom you really did not want to let down. She was elegant and very clever, quite elderly (so it seemed at the time – she was only in her fifties!), softly spoken, but most definitely in charge. Once when I was sent to her for yet another minor misdemeanour, she quite undid me, not by scolding, but by being disappointed. She epitomized for me the kind of strong, magnetic woman I wanted to be. Maybe there are echoes of her in my character now, but I'm nowhere near as calm and poised.

She was also a woman with a strong Christian faith and a vivid sense of social responsibility. She was carrying on a long-established tradition, set down by the great Victorian educator Frances Mary Buss, the school's founder. It might be couched in different terms now, and I know that private schools are seen by many as a cause for scorn, but the view was that we were privileged members of society, and therefore it was our duty to use that privilege for the good of others. So we would host an annual Christmas party for a local home for the severely disabled, there would be numerous charity collections and events through the year, and in the sixth form we were all expected to undertake voluntary work in one form or another. I helped out at a local old folks' home with some of my classmates, singing songs, chatting, listening. It probably *was* a bit patronizing, but it did establish in me a sense of obligation, and of how even small gestures could make a big difference to one person. I remember one occasion when representatives from the John Groom's charity laid on an event whereby we could all experience just a fraction of the physical challenges posed by being in a wheelchair. As we struggled our way around the netball court, trying to pick up small items with a grabber, I had my eyes opened. All part of an education in empathy I suppose, although the Christian ethos was little more than a generalized moral framework for me at the time.

We were of an era when there was still a Christian assembly every day, although the sizeable group of Jewish pupils had a separate Jewish assembly in the gym. It was all very mysterious to us Gentile girls, especially as we were banned from attending.

Assembly usually included a music student playing something worthy on the violin or organ, followed by a rousing hymn, presided over by the large and enthusiastic Miss G., a former opera singer. We were encouraged to enunciate correctly:

"It's 'We plough the fields and scetter', gels, not 'sca-a-atter.'"

Then the Head would read something improving – and quite often that would be an excerpt from John Bunyan's famous work from the seventeenth century, *The Pilgrim's Progress*. Bunyan was clearly a bit of a favourite of the Headmistress, and of our school's eminent founder too – even the school song was Bunyan's hymn, "He who would valiant be". It's funny that Reverend Bunyan should have become such a marker of respectability, because in his day he was a bit of a scallywag, and went around upsetting the good burghers of Bedfordshire with his non-conformist preaching. In those days to attend anything other than a Church of England service was a criminal offence, and so he was incarcerated several times in Bedford Gaol from the 1660s onwards. He wouldn't give up though, and in time, as the law and attitudes changed, Bunyan was granted significant civil and church roles. Quite a turnaround for a repeat offender!

I still shake my head in amused wonder at the coincidence (or maybe it's more…) that having been steeped in Bunyan as a teenager, I should now, as an adult, find myself the representative of Christianity in Bedford Prison. However, despite the strong historical link, the building you see today is not on the same site. The current HMP Bedford was built in 1801, on St Loyes Street, at the northern end of the town. There have been a number of additions since, with the modern gatehouse completing the frontage in 1990.

From the street it's a substantial and fairly imposing building, with enormous gates that open occasionally to reveal a dark and cavernous vehicle entrance area. I wonder what men sitting inside the sweatbox (the colloquial name for the prison van) think as they look out and see it for the first time, especially those who've never been to prison before. It is a bit different to that first view of my privileged and rather lovely school.

Still, I've been surprised at the number of people who've remarked that they never realized there was a prison in Bedford, or at least had no idea where it was. This seems to reinforce my view that, in general, we don't really want to know what happens on the other side of the wall. It's as if there's a collective blind spot, and in fact that blind spot seems to extend to the staff working behind those walls as well as those committed by the courts. Mark Richards, a prison officer interviewed by the BBC in 2007, said: "We are the forgotten service. The police are visible; we are not. We are behind walls and no one knows what goes on."

Inevitably there's going to be an air of mystery, because

the Prison Service can't just open its doors and welcome everyone in. So media opportunities are carefully scrutinized, and the interests of security, as well as victim sensitivity, quite properly must guide much of the message. I have had to work long and hard to gain the trust of governors and the authorities in London, who allow me to continue with my media career. Still I have to tread the fine line between an honest representation of what I do, and putting out there, however inadvertently, something which compromises safety, security or matters which are rightly confidential. I'm employed by the Prison Service, not the church, so I'm a civil servant, subject to the Official Secrets Act and all the other expectations of a Crown employee.

But I do have a real concern with the seemingly large numbers of people who don't want to engage with the realities of life behind bars, beyond the sweeping statements of "It's all a holiday camp anyway." Nurses and police are, quite rightly and deservedly, lauded for their work, and their rights to decent pay and conditions are defended robustly. But once the police have captured and processed an offender, once the ambulance workers have scraped them off the streets, and the nurses have patched up the violent and the drunk, where do they go? Who deals with the very same difficult – often dangerous – individuals? And who has the unenviable task, in the face of scarce resources, of trying to turn these individuals into integrated, law-abiding, responsible members of the society into which they will inevitably be released?

And that's before you turn to the individuals themselves, who must repay their debt to society by losing their liberty. I'm no apologist for wrong-doing, and due punishment must be served. But *someone* has to engage with offenders on a level that goes deep enough to discover the mess of emotion, anger, and experience that has produced the levels of irresponsibility, violence, and addiction paving the road to jail.

This is exactly what I try to do, alongside colleagues of all disciplines. It's those early days of mine that set me off – but not the privilege, nor the education. Instead it was family difficulties, my personal sense of dislocation from an early age, and some unhappy days, overlaid by the duty inculcated in me by those marvellous ladies of learning. It's also the knowledge that if it had not been for my own discovery of faith, I could easily have trodden a similar path to many of those I meet in jail.

FAMILY (MIS)FORTUNES

We prison chaplains have to be a circumspect bunch. Quite often we'll take a phone call from a woman connected to a prisoner, who tells us she's his girlfriend. We're expected to check out all information received, so into the computer system we go, looking for the relatives and contacts listed there – often to find that there are three or four "girlfriends" listed against an individual prisoner, as well as a wife! I've had the experience of telling a prisoner his girlfriend rang, only to be asked "Which one?" and the phrase "babymother" (meaning the mother of a prisoner's baby, but not necessarily his girlfriend or wife) is used frequently without so much as a flinch. Family relationships are complicated, often volatile and unstable, and a veritable minefield. Little wonder we have to be cautious.

That habitual circumspection is there for serious security reasons too. We might be taking a phone call from someone the prisoner isn't supposed to contact – maybe there's an injunction, but the caller chooses, for whatever reason, to ignore it. Or even public protection issues may be involved. I have had situations where a girlfriend has rung in, and in fact she's the victim of the crime – on a couple of occasions she was underage as well. Although this might sound odd, some women do try to maintain contact in these circumstances. Sometimes this is a by-product of how deeply they have been abused and brainwashed; at other times they appear to me simply to have no real understanding of their own vulnerability. We always have to be on our guard and can't take anything at face value.

Several times a week we'll receive a call from the outside telling us that a relative of a serving prisoner has died. It's our job to go and find said prisoner, sit him down, and break the news. Clearly, that's difficult news to give, and even harder to receive. One of the things that prison unceremoniously removes is all control over your personal life. Those aspects you take for granted – such as being able to have as much contact with your family as you want or need, as frequently as you wish – are simply not there. So it's a delicate task, helping a prisoner negotiate the emotional minefield of bereavement during their incarceration.

But this is where the circumspection comes in again. Check, check, and check again. Over time it's become part of accepted practice that a prison chaplain, receiving news of a relative's death, has to check it out first. That means ringing the hospital, doctor, social worker, police officer, and obtaining independent verification of the death, before breaking the news. Why? Because whilst it is infrequent, it isn't unheard of for a friend or family member to ring in with information which turns out to be totally untrue. It might be a mistake – families are far apart, rumour mills work overtime; but it can be a coded message, or an attempt to get at the offender and cause pain and distress. If you're going to tell someone devastating news, with all the potential ramifications for their well-being, you need to make sure it's accurate news.

Complex family issues are familiar territory in jail, and some of the stories you hear could break your heart. When I first turned to prison ministry, I started out as a chaplain in a Secure Training Centre (a facility for 12–17-year-olds). The youngest resident I met was twelve years old, a boy: let's call him Sam. He had a history of offending – minor stuff at first, shoplifting, criminal damage, but this had escalated and now Sam had turned violent and seemingly uncontrollable. I was shocked when I first met him, because he was a small, skinny boy, with an open face and big eyes, only a year older than my son. I sat with him and chatted a bit about his path to secure accommodation. He'd been kicked out of school, was living with foster parents, saw his mum occasionally, but she was a drug addict. He had no idea about his father, but had an older brother who was also a tearaway, and Sam had initially stolen from shops because there was no one at home to feed him. Inevitably he had fallen in with an older crowd, who used his naivety and desire to belong for their own ends. Not that he was naïve any longer, of course. But I saw a little boy who was lost, sad, confused, and desperate to cover it all up with bravado, lashing out at the world which seemed to have failed him so completely. I later discovered that Sam had to undergo a "catch up" immunization programme because he had not even had the basic vaccinations he needed as a baby, such was the situation he had been born into.

It's never an excuse for wrongdoing, but this kind of story is all too familiar to me these days. Grown men sob as they tell me about the beatings (and worse) they suffered, multiple bereavements, living in fear. They have spent their early adolescence not only trying to fathom the inevitable inner confusions, but doing it against a backdrop of domestic violence, addictions, poverty, and abuse. Bewildering family relationships, mental ill-health, and educational failure: in one way or another, they've missed out on the essential building blocks that create the stable foundation of a person's life. Research tells us that the early years are the ones which write the disk, and although after that the encoding can be amended to a degree, it can never be overwritten completely. Those early experiences will cast a shadow for the rest of someone's life, although they can learn to recognize, live with, and minimize the effects.

I should know.

I once had to help my son create a family tree for his school homework – it was so complex it looked more like a diagram for an extensive heating system! There were step-fathers, half-brothers, and wayward figures, liberally sprinkled with grudges, rival factions, and years of radio silence.

I was born in the mid-60s and spent my early years in Hampshire and then Guildford. My immediate family was my mother, father, and brother: nice and simple. Sadly Mum and Dad divorced when I was nine. It was a bit unusual back then but not exactly outrageous. Mother remarried: enter stepfather, new family unit. This marriage wasn't a happy one, and it ended about a decade later. Mother eventually married yet again. By today's standards, what's the issue? In fact, I am now married for the third time myself, so I'm not one to judge.

Except.

For many reasons I was deeply unsettled and unhappy as a child and a teenager. I often felt unloved, unlovable, and sometimes even unsafe. I was not able to communicate this to anyone, and as the years went by, I became more and more lonely and distressed. There was no Childline in those days – although how ironic is it that Dame Esther Rantzen (its founder) is an old girl from my school and I even used her history book in the Upper Fourths? A long life later, I no longer have any anger or bitterness left about those unhappy days, but there's no doubt they left their mark on me.

Mother loomed so large that my Dad wasn't given space to be a towering influence when I was little. He was out at work; although I have happy memories of days out with him driving us around the summer countryside, often finding a hidden pub on the way home for a bottle of the fizzy stuff and a bag of crisps. He was a big cuddly man, good at cricket, calm. I felt safe when he was around. Once he and Mum split up I saw him at weekends, in fact he even lived with us again for a while, but it wasn't until I left home for university that I managed to re-establish our relationship properly. Since then he's been the proverbial rock and we've had many a night comparing notes about the old days.

One really positive relationship back then was with my maternal grandparents. I loved them to bits, and remember many happy summer days with them in the Gloucestershire countryside. They came across as settled, happy people – at least to the childish me. It was from my grandmother I learned the love of the countryside, and via Grandad I learned the rules of rugby!

I find that the men in prison often have a better relationship with their grandparents than their parents too, especially their "Nan". Grandmothers seem to be more solid, more present, for these men, than their mothers are able to be, and often it's Nan who has effectively brought them up. Is that simply the responsibility of maturity, or is it something about being one generation removed and able to reflect on your own mistakes?

But that one-step removal can be a problem for prisoners. If a grandparent dies while someone's in jail, there's no guarantee of the prisoner being able to attend the funeral, unless it can be proven that the grandparent served as a parent. I'm often asked to give talks to community groups about the experience of being in prison and the issue of funerals is one I use to emphasize the extent of what is lost once you go inside. I ask people to raise their hand if they've had a friend or family member die in the preceding twelve months. Given the demographic of the groups I talk to there are usually quite a lot of hands in the air. I then ask how many of them had to ask permission to attend the funeral. All the hands go down and there is an exchange of some puzzled looks. I explain that all prisoners must apply for permission to attend the funeral of a relative or friend. That's after the chaplain has verified that the news of the death is bona fide.

Permission is in the hands of the governor, who must take into account security issues (Will there be hundreds at the funeral and is there an escape or assault risk?); staffing (Do I have two prison officers available to escort this prisoner – who will be cuffed to them – and are they at risk in any way?); public protection (Are there child protection issues, or harassment charges, who will be there?); victims of the original crime; public perception (the so-called "tabloid test") and even whether the prisoner is physically and mentally fit to attend. Even if all of these come up as satisfactory, often it's only the funeral of a first-line relative (parent, child, sibling, spouse) which is allowable.

If they can't attend, the chapel is made available for the prisoner – whatever their faith. They can say prayers, light a candle, speak with their chaplain. Even if they do go to the funeral, pastoral follow-up is essential. We're not good at dealing with death in our society, and a funeral can be a distressing event for anyone. Prison staff will be on the lookout for any excessive signs of distress that might lead to conflict with others, an episode of self-harm or even a suicide attempt. Generally speaking, prisoners are very good at supporting one another in these circumstances – so many have suffered more than one bereavement, and can really share the experience. There are also Listeners (Samaritan-trained peers) who are often called upon in the dark watches of the night when there's time – too much time – to think.

It's often a death that will set a man off down the road of self-reflection. How did I get to this point in my life? What else will I lose and how can I get out of this? I find that the younger men, say those aged between eighteen and thirty, are the hardest to work with, pastorally, as they're still at the bravado stage. They're less likely to reflect, and more likely to "act out" their anger and pain. But hit the thirties, and especially towards the forties, and men do begin to question what they're doing with their lives. Perhaps their own children are growing up, or their partner has finally left them. That grandparent dies, they understand their own physical strength will wane one day, and amidst the wreckage suddenly all the big questions rear up.

Helping someone make sense of all this takes time, and a lot of listening skills. It's a fairly common misconception that the chaplains are there to throw religion at you, but in fact only a relatively small proportion of what we do is about religious practice. More often we are spending patient hours walking with someone through the tangled jungle of his years, helping him find his own pathway out into the light.

I've found my own life experiences to be hugely helpful in this. I don't make a big deal of them but they're not a secret either. It's not the done thing to share your own troubles, past or otherwise, with someone you're supporting, but it certainly informs your responses. It is important though, to separate your own experience from the man in front of you – there's all the dangers of trying to fight your own demons by battling someone else's.

When Greg asked to come to the chapel on the day of his Nan's funeral, I didn't think anything of it. He came, we lit the candle, I said the prayers. As usual, I stayed for a chat, and his story came tumbling out. His oppressive, critical mother and his sense of failure; his longing for a better life and his shame at his crime, fuelled by an addiction to drugs, which he took to numb the inner pain he felt. And then he told me that at the age of seventeen he'd discovered that the man he'd always thought was his uncle was in fact his father and his supposed father was no blood relation at all. He broke down in tears. As he sobbed, the full force of his identity crisis shook him and he was once again the lost kid without a clue who he was or where he belonged.

A long time later I took Greg back to his cell, and then shut myself away in my office with a strong cup of tea. This one was close to the bone.

When I was coming up to O levels (as they were then) school told us to bring in our birth certificates so they could verify our correct name and date of birth. I duly went home and asked for mine. Apparently it had been lost ages ago so I was furnished with a letter verifying my personal details instead. That satisfied the school but like most teenagers I didn't like feeling different. So a few days later, when I was alone in the house, I'm afraid I went snooping. Heart thumping, I found a box at the bottom of a wardrobe. There was my birth certificate. I hesitated for a moment – what was the big secret? I was expecting to find a weird middle name, or maybe that my parents weren't married when I was born. As I unfolded the evidence of my origins, nothing could have prepared my 14-year-old self for the earthquake that hit me. No weird names, the mother and father married. But the name of my father was not the man I had known as Dad my whole life.

I kept my discovery to myself. I didn't dare confess to my snooping and couldn't even begin to contemplate the consequences of laying bare the revelation. I don't think I could have felt more alone. The phrase kept swirling round my head – "who are you?" It did make sense of a really early flash of memory I'd had some years before – a memory of a long dark-panelled room, my mother in a blue suit, flowers, me dressed up, and lots of people having a party. Some time later I saw a picture of my mother's (second) wedding – that memory was accurate.

But now the whole chronology of my life shifted. Being 14 was already demanding enough – exams, an emotional holocaust at home, hormones dancing a merry jig – but this? This I just buried, and lived with the thought that I belonged nowhere, and had just lost the bit of my life I thought I could trust.

I did a lot of burying during my formative years – interring anger, confusion, pain. I learned to lie – not only at home for self-protection, but to my school friends as well – inventing a life that was happy, sociable, normal. And the stories I told myself were just as untrue, although I've only come to realize that as I've healed. I told myself I was unlovable, that I was alone, that I was ugly, stupid, a waste of space.

All these emotions I encounter on a frequent basis amongst the men I support. I had the advantage of a first-class education, and at least the strict rules at home kept me off the streets (although, as we'll see, being let loose at university is another story…). I also turned my despair and confusion into an independence and bloody-mindedness which has served me well. But if I'd lived in poverty, or been a young man in a gang-infested area; if I'd skipped school or run away…

In fact I did get close to running away that summer I was fourteen. Living in North London I was a "Gooner" and idolized the Arsenal team of the early 80s – Pat Jennings, Liam Brady, David O'Leary. Somehow, I reckoned, I needed to get away from home and the only place I could think of to go was Highbury – home of my heroes. Quite what I thought I'd do once I got there, I have no idea! I sneaked some spare clothes and a chocolate bar into my school bag, and instead of going to registration, I changed out of my uniform, and walked across Canons Park to the Tube station. I even bought a ticket to Highbury. But once on the platform I saw sense – I'd be found, hauled back, and life would be even worse. So I trudged back across the park and even made it into school in time for lesson one. Huh. I couldn't even manage to run away properly!

CHAPTER 3

SAVING GRACES

One of the "saving graces" during my teenage years was discovering karate. At the age of sixteen, I'd taken up a part-time job in a local pharmacy, and had hit it off with the pharmacist and his wife. Kind, funny, intelligent, a loving family, they were the adult role models I needed to restore a bit of my faith in the world. And they were karate nuts. Eventually they persuaded me to go along, and I loved it! Within eighteen months, I was reaching the higher grades and had been awarded the club's Student of the Year award. The club, and its members of all ages, taught me self-discipline, brought me friendships (even my first boyfriend) and helped me to survive the final couple of years at home, together with the stress of A levels and university applications.

My pharmacist friend knew a lot about my home situation, and one night, after yet another awful event, I remember him telling me to look to the future for myself, not for anyone else, to get my head down, work hard and get through, because it would be my ticket out and away. He was right in lots of ways, although finding true "freedom" was to take many more years.

We can go a long way if we have a focus point, a reason to strive and go forward. We also need the hope that our striving will pay off. Lacking either, or both, of these would have sunk me, as it sinks so many.

Ray was a high-profile offender whom I got to know through daily rounds on the healthcare wing of a High Security establishment. I was a junior member of the chaplaincy team, unburdened by management or administration, so I had time to sit and listen. I really enjoyed these daily rounds – known as the "stats", or statutory duties: a visit to the healthcare inpatients wing, to the segregation unit, and to the First Night Centre. Anything could come up – a young man newly sentenced and panicking; an old hand trying to blag an extra phone call; someone lost in a labyrinth of mental illness; or a humorous encounter with a bunch of real characters.

Ray was one of the very few prisoners I've dealt with who I thought was probably a lost cause. He was in his late thirties, he'd committed a terribly violent and random crime, and had just received an extremely long sentence. Listening to his life story, he was quite clearly a very damaged man, and, once again, it was his early years that had laid the foundation for his disintegration. He had found no hope, no friend, no reason to strive. Nothing had given him a lifeline, and although he was very intelligent, he had entered adulthood with the view that nobody wanted him, so he would want nobody in return. You hear the phrase "something inside just died" and it's a cliché. But when I looked at Ray, that phrase rang true. There was no light in his eyes, no sense of a soul behind the mask. I'm not a medic, but I suppose as a layperson I might call him a psychopath – utterly cut off from the rest of the world. He self-harmed unbelievably – deep, vicious cuts to his arms, which he enjoyed displaying to gauge a reaction. Quite how, as a young chaplain, I didn't flinch when I saw bone beneath his dressing I'll never know. You don't tend to see that on *The Vicar of Dibley*.

Having committed the crime that would finally see him inside for probably the rest of his natural life, Ray's view was that he would kill himself eventually, because that was the logical thing to do. He had no one, he said, had nothing to offer the world, wanted nothing from the world, had no remorse, had no feelings at all. His continued existence served no purpose to himself or anyone else.

I tried all the "good vicar" things – you can change yourself, you can learn to reflect and review what you have done, you can still make a contribution, even from inside. But with this man I didn't really believe it and neither did he. I had to face the fact that here was a seemingly utterly lost soul – and his logic was probably right. This was one I'd have to leave to powers far higher than me…

I don't know what happened to Ray, if he's still alive, or if things have changed for him. But it was a hard and painful string of encounters – and a reminder that there isn't always a happy ending, or even potential for one. At times like these, my role as a chaplain isn't to work for change with someone. It isn't to steer their thoughts to a different future. It's more just to "accompany" someone for the time they are in my care.

You can't help but wonder about some of the prisoners after you, or they, have moved on. There are times when you work with someone at a very personal level, being trusted with their deepest fears and regrets, hopes and longings, often at points of real crisis. I recall several occasions when I've sat on the floor of a constant watch cell with a prisoner, because that's where he is sitting, and listened as he tried to unravel the knotted mess of his situation. Sometimes my staying with a prisoner and letting him talk has probably stopped him killing himself. Other times I've gone home and worried half the night whether another prisoner would be there in the morning.

A prisoner can't become a friend – that would be a serious breach of security and could leave an individual very vulnerable indeed – but you do sometimes make a connection. In fact, I question whether a chaplain can minister properly to someone if they don't make some sort of link with them. Most of the time the criminal justice system and society dehumanize offenders. They become a kind of caricature: a thief, an addict, a killer. I think we do it because it helps us to distance ourselves from their crimes, as if by making the criminals less than human we don't have to face the potential for similar behaviour in ourselves.

Until fairly recently it was still prison practice to address a convicted criminal only by his surname, or even just by his prison number. Now, acknowledging the psychological benefit of making those connections, we are required to call them "Mr So and So", or to use their first name. I know there are officers (and members of the public) who lament this, thinking it's soft, but I don't think someone is going to learn to treat others as human beings with rights and feelings if they are not treated that way themselves. I believe we have to model the behaviour we are expecting and we have to find the human being behind the crime if we are to address what has happened. We won't always succeed, as I couldn't with Ray, but sometimes we will.

In that same High Security jail I also used to visit the closed supervision unit – the prison within a prison where the most serious offenders lived. I think I was a source of some amusement at first, amongst the officers and residents. Here I was, an attractive young woman, turning up in a dog collar and having coffee with some of the most dangerous men in the country. "Ey-up, here's the God Squad," was one officer's regular greeting. Here, more than anywhere, I didn't really expect to change anyone or achieve a great deal. I felt completely out of my depth. But I still felt it was important to go once a week.

It was an intimidating place, behind its own high walls. Entry was centrally controlled, cameras were everywhere, and there was an unsettling quiet atmosphere, especially on the units where only one man was allowed out at a time. I went to each of the small inner units. Sometimes I delivered a Bible or a holy book for a different faith. I'd stop and have a chat, ask about a family issue, joke about something in the newspaper: all trivial human interaction in a cold and sterile environment. Occasionally I'd be sworn at. More often I would be ignored. Sometimes a conversation would give me the creeps and I'd be very glad for the presence of my uniformed colleagues, who were never more than a few paces away.

On one wing there was a man who wanted me to take him Holy Communion. The first time I did so, I turned up with my little Communion case, Bible, and priest's stole. "Hold on a minute," the supervising officer said. "We're just getting the room ready." Officers were removing almost every scrap of furniture from a long glass-fronted room until at last there was only a table with a chair either side of it remaining. The prisoner was shown in and instructed to sit on the chair on the far side of the table, thus putting an obstacle in between him and me. He was facing the glass front of the room; I had my back to it. The officers left the room and I began to lay out the items for communion. As I glanced over my shoulder I saw the supervising officer and no less than *five* other officers standing in a row on the other side of the glass, arms folded, watching proceedings. It was all for my own safety, of course, but it was a bizarre way to conduct a religious ceremony.

One of the units in this close supervision centre was for men who had to be isolated from others for their own protection – often because they had grassed up co-defendants, thus putting their lives in danger. One man I visited on this unit, let's call him Danny, was a former gangster who had done just that and in fact was now part of a protected witness scheme. He had to change his name, had been given new identity documents, and knew there was a price on his head. I got to know him simply by sitting down for a coffee with him and the other unit residents. We'd make small talk about the fish in the fish tank that they were allowed to have, or take the mickey out of whichever resident was on cooking duty for the day. Occasionally we'd comment on something in the papers (although I tended to try to avoid that, as it was usually page three they were most interested in…). There was week after week of seemingly useless, pointless trivia, in which I kept the conversation going even though it was stilted. I was determined to break the stereotype of a chaplain as a naïve and delicate flower. The other officers were clearly laughing at me, albeit not unkindly.

And then one day Danny looked up when I came on the unit and said, "Can we have a private chat?" Another glass-fronted room, not such a hefty uniformed presence, but a watchful eye nonetheless. He wanted my advice about how to deal with his father, who was coming to visit him for the first time in many years, and who had been diagnosed with terminal cancer. It was all the more complicated as Danny was being set up with a new life after his release, which was due the following year. So this might also be the last time he would ever see his father.

We talked about repentance and forgiveness, about human frailty, about hope even in the worst of circumstances. I didn't try to give him easy answers, or in fact any answers – how could I? But listening to him, giving him space to be himself, rather than just a "badass gangster", was restoring to him, perhaps, a little of his humanity – and that is what I was there to do.

He met his father, there were hard words, there were tears, there was, finally, a hug and a handshake. Danny's father died a month later.

Over the ensuing months I visited Danny every week. We spoke about his offending, his family, his regrets, his fears. He asked for Holy Communion and I brought it. Not once did he ask me to write him a good report, or do anything for him. He wasn't using religion to curry favour.

Danny began to find a focus and some hope. He got into trouble less on the unit, became more co-operative, more respectful. Shortly before I left that prison he told me his real name. It was a gesture of connection I shall never forget – and although he wrote to me at my new place of work once, after his release, thanking me for staying by his side, telling me he'd found a partner, and was even attending church, it was that moment of self-revealing that convinced me he had a future, and would make something different of his life.

Two decades earlier, I'd had high hopes for my future too, when I turned up at university one October day in the early 80s. Finally free of home's oppressive atmosphere, I was looking forward to the chance to make something of *my* life, getting my teeth into study, and adult freedom. But having lived this peculiar combination of a harsh but sheltered life, in fact I was terribly vulnerable. So here's another "first day", at the start of a first week, which culminated in the Freshers' Ball. And a salutary lesson for one naïve undergraduate who came to understand that the fellow who showed so much interest, bought drinks all night (with the inevitable effect on me), walked me back to halls and then expected his due, was not going to become a boyfriend, but was actually participating in the game of "Bag a Fresher".

I was introduced to a fair number of games in the next couple of years, many of them involving sexual coercion, and a fair few involving drugs. I fell for it every time. Any boy who glanced my way was going to be my handsome prince, and more than once I was used terribly by a young man who I thought would love me but in fact was gone by the next day. I had no framework for understanding how relationships worked, I had rock-bottom self-esteem, and I was hungry for attention and affection. And, unfortunately, I also discovered alcohol and weed. Desperate to fit in (again), and with very little sense of personal value, soon the lectures were kicked into touch, whispers about me grew nasty, and when yet another row with my mother resulted in me being told not to come home one day at the end of a Spring term, I was homeless as well.

Things were not looking promising at this point – the ill-advised behaviour was putting me in physical danger, and also had the potential for criminal involvement (although, thankfully, I never actually stepped over that line). My mental health was shaky as well.

Most of the prisoners I've worked with have had issues with drugs or alcohol. They might be inside for violence, for theft, for reckless driving, murder or rape. But probably eight times out of ten, there's a history of drug-taking or too much booze. I can see how easy it is to get started – after all, I did. I'd had the miserable childhood, buried anger and distress, and a lack of personal boundaries. Add to that the problems I didn't have – poverty, poor housing, no prospects, failed education, and traumatic bereavements – faced with that most of us would want to bury our battered souls in something or other. Almost every addicted man I talk to has deep personal damage tucked away, damage usually done by the time he was ten. If the dealers are hanging around on your street corner, if the lads you idolize tell you it's OK, or even threaten you if you don't join in… and then, once you're in it's very hard to get out again. Anyone who's ever tried to give up smoking, or even chocolate, knows the truth of that.

My tutor managed to find me emergency digs, and so I spent the holidays revising for exams, manically exercising (I was still into the karate) and limiting my food intake to one yoghurt a day. In this I was like many other young women who punish themselves to deal with distress. I was also still trying to come to terms with the identity crisis triggered at fourteen, so I'd turn up to lectures one day dressed in frills and looking very ladylike, and then the next I'd be sporting black leather, heavy eyeliner and spikey hair. In many ways I lived the whole adolescent rebellion thing in the space of three years. My tutors had the patience of saints, and I'm amazed that not only did I not get pregnant/a disease/ arrested/thrown out, but after three years I came away with a second-class law degree.

I have to say that the relatively positive outcome was thanks to the combination of three men – in no particular order: my dad (the cuddly, calm one, not the late-discovered biological father), the boyfriend whom I later married, and a two-thousand-year-old bloke with a beard and sandals (allegedly).

For a long, long time I didn't tell Dad what I'd discovered about my parentage. I didn't want to hurt him, and I'd seen him suffer enough as a result of the breakdown of his marriage to my mother. The fact that he maintained contact with me over the years and tried to provide consistent loving support when I got to university, even though he knew the truth for himself, is a testament to the remarkable man he is. It was very difficult to have any relationship with him whilst I was a teenager, but once I was away from home it took very little time for the bonds to grow. He did for me what I suppose I now try to do as a chaplain – he provided a non-judgmental *presence*, that "accompanying" I've spoken about. Allowing me space to take my own decisions, make my own mistakes, but always being ready for the time when I needed to reflect, cry or yell "Help!" My main mistake during those crazy years was not making use of his wisdom soon enough – it might have saved me a fair bit of anguish.

A regular feature of student life was the Students' Union Bar. Sprawled across the back of an ugly 1960s concrete block, the Nelson Mandela Bar had a low ceiling, a raised area in the middle hosting some lumpy armchairs, and a space at one end for the inevitable student bands. The carpet was grubby and nondescript and the place seemed dark even in the middle of the day. But come the evening, when it was full of New Romantics and post-punks, with Flock of Seagulls haircuts and Gary Numan eyeliner, this dingy common room became a place of magic and promise, a chance to discover and display one's inner cool to the throbbing soundtrack of Spandau Ballet. Or at least that's what we thought.

We had plenty of headline names play in our main hall – the Stranglers, A-ha, the Communards (Richard Coles and I both in our pre-vicar days). On the other hand, the student bar was a bit like the indie fringe. Here hopefuls from among the residents would strut their stuff, no doubt hoping success might one day render unnecessary the daytime drudge of lectures and seminars. One night in my second year I was quite taken with a covers band on stage. In truth I was quite taken with the guitarist. They were playing two one-hour sets, and in between these I manage to wangle an introduction to both the guitarist (tall, blond, charismatic, *guitarist!*) and the drummer (not so tall, quiet, geeky). Alas, it soon emerged that the guitarist was happily ensconced with a long-term girlfriend. He wandered off to the bar, leaving me with the geeky drummer.

He turned out to be an absolute charmer, witty and amusing to boot. We talked for ages, and once they returned to the stage, I spent the rest of the evening watching the intricacies of percussion for the first time in my life.

A delightful few months ensued, until some silly spat got in the way. I flounced off, drama-queen style, and that was that. It was back to the old ways, the disaster-filled encounters, and the ever-descending spiral. Not that I was sitting in a room somewhere sobbing my heart out. I was having a *whale* of a time, on the outside at least. But I was lonely, I had very few friends, and no appetite for my law course, which bored me to tears. I moved from one set of grotty digs to another, got glandular fever over the summer which meant I couldn't get a job, and I simply drifted from one party to the next – where I was never one of the in-crowd, but always an outsider.

About a year later I bumped into him again. In the time since I'd seen him, he'd undergone quite a change, seeming now much happier, more sorted. Several late-night conversations in the pub revealed the source of this new-found equilibrium:

the guy had found God. And yet, reassuringly, he still liked a pint, retained his cool fashion sense, and still played the drums. Intrigued, I resolved secretly to visit his local church to see if it was all he had cracked it up to be.

The Church of St John and St Stephen was octagonal, modern, set in the middle of a run-down social housing estate. It nestled in a dip, with a paved area in front, the trees and shrubs planted in the middle of this area giving the impression of stillness despite the unforgiving environment. I was dressed smartly in preparation for the ten o'clock service, in a black and white printed skirt, white blouse, black velvet jacket, and low court heels. This was both unusual for me and a major mistake. Having planned to slip in unobtrusively and sit at the back, I edged through the heavy double doors into the light and airy lobby only to be greeted enthusiastically by a smiling woman clutching leaflets and clad in… jeans. Inside a further set of wooden doors I could hear music – not an organ, but a piano, guitars, drums for goodness' sake! In I went, and all hope of blending in was dashed as even the older members of the gathered congregation appeared to be in bright, casual clothing. So much for my stereotypical view of churchgoers.

I survived the morning service, even quite liked it if I'm honest, and was touched by the number of people who came up to me to pass on a word of welcome, but without being pushy or nosey. As I was leaving, polite young woman that I was, I shook the dashing young curate's hand, and muttered something about having enjoyed myself and thank you very much.

"Lovely!" he exclaimed, "So pleased to welcome you. There's a healing service on here at 6 p.m. if you come back – I think you might like that too."

I made my escape and walked the quarter mile or so back to my student accommodation. My housemates were lying around in the communal sitting room when I arrived back.

"You coming down the Fisherman's tonight Shaz?" asked Fi. Without thinking, I replied, "No, I'm going to church."

How could I know that turning up at 6 p.m. was going to change my life for ever? It's incredible, when we look back, how there are seminal moments – but we so rarely see them coming. Just as we slip and slide into the quagmires little by little, destruction by degree, hardly recognizing the path we're on, so we can be presented with the means of our rescue in such an ordinary way. I returned to church that sunny Sunday evening because of the former boyfriend, the woman at the door, the family who said hello, the young clergyman who invited me, something in my own subconscious. It was completely banal. And yet... what did Hamlet say? "There's a divinity that shapes our ends/ Rough-hew them how we will."

There was some lovely music playing, some singing of simple repetitive chants, prayers, and words with a Celtic feel. We were all sat in a kind of circle arrangement, and I'd managed to put myself fairly near the back, near a pillar. It was all very lovely, and quite peaceful in the dim lighting.

"I'd like you to sit quietly for a moment now," instructed the vicar, a friendly looking chap in his fifties, wearing vicar robes but coming across as very unstuffy. "Then if you would like to have someone pray for you, for healing of any sort, please come forward."

"Not on your nelly," I thought.

"If you don't want to come forward," Mr Vicar continued, "then you can simply kneel where you are and someone will come and pray with you there."

The pianist started playing a tinkly tune and I settled back to watch the poor saps who believed in this sort of stuff, toddling up to get a blessing or whatever.

Which is when I felt the hand on my back, gently pushing. "Get off!" I thought, turning around, ready to give the owner of the intruding hand a piece of my mind. Except the row behind me was empty.

Turning back, I shook my head, shrugged my shoulders. There it was again, gentle, but insistent. And then suddenly, spookily, another invisible pressure on my chest, pushing the opposite way. "Wha-at?"

For what can only have been seconds, but felt like an age, these two "hands" effectively battled it out, and I was aware of sitting there, rocking, like something out of *One Flew Over the Cuckoo's Nest*. Forwards, backwards – it was a physical sensation.

And then forwards won. I found myself on my knees where I had been sitting. I had a very bodily sense of being emptied out (a bit like a case of violent diarrhoea, without the unpleasant results). At the same time I was aware of a rushing in of warmth and light, and at some deep level I knew, just knew, it was a spiritual experience. I'd call it God now, but at the time I didn't even need to name what was happening – I could tell it was a turning point. I say I was aware – I was in some ways, but in other ways this seemed to be happening to me in another zone, and I was on the outside observing. I realized I was crying and then gradually became aware of real people either side of me, muttering under their breath, I presume praying. All I could say, amidst my tears, was "Thank you, thank you."

That day really did change so much. In the weeks that followed I altered my habits, reconnected with my studies, and regained a boyfriend. As I've gone on in ministry I've tended to wince at my colleagues who pepper their conversation with "Jesus this" and "The Lord that". It's been interesting to see the renewed debate about whether "Christian-speak" is embarrassing for those on the receiving end – er… yes, it is, in my opinion. As a result, sometimes the producer on *Pause for Thought* tells me I'm not being religious enough. Prison has taught me to tread gently with the religious imagery and buzzwords and it's not my style anyway. But make no mistake, I have a profound admiration for Jesus, and the things he taught – as well as a deep sense that there is so much more to this life and world than we can ever imagine.

I have to admit I also have a hefty chunk of cynicism about the Church and often despair at the harshness and judgmentalism of many who call themselves faithful. But I go back to my own experience of conversion many times, especially when work or life has got me down, and I'm questioning what I do or why. Not quite twenty years old, I was in a mess, and couldn't have foreseen that evening's events nor their far-reaching consequences. If it can happen for me it can happen for others. Maybe not so dramatically, nor so instantly: the road to faith can be a long and winding one, with false starts, stumbles, slips backwards, and wrong turns. So can the road to rebuilding a life after prison. My hope is that my experiences can help a few set their feet on the road to at least one, if not both, of these destinations.

HIGHWAY TO HOPE

Life in prison is regulated by an extensive collection of Prison Service Instructions or PSIs. They range from rules about prisoner clothing to how staff may (or may not) engage with the media, from detailed frameworks for education to requirements for searching visitors. It's a quasi-military structure in many ways, with a strong hierarchical flavour, and feels a world apart from the outside. Prisons are inspected regularly but unexpectedly by Her Majesty's Inspector of Prisons ("HMIP are in the area" being a phrase to strike dread into the heart of most senior managers), and many areas and disciplines within the establishment are also subject to a demanding regime of audits and compliance tests. Score anything lower than the ninetieth percentile and the overall rating for the prison is affected, with subsequent hard questions asked of the governor. There is a sense of constant pressure to achieve the required standard – not necessarily a bad thing in itself, as keeping custody of others is a huge responsibility – but in the middle of an inspection, or with an upcoming audit, there's plenty of sleep lost and many a frayed temper.

Chaplains are part of this too, and have their very own PSI, setting out mandatory tasks and expectations. Each chaplaincy team receives an annual Compliance and Assurance visit (effectively an audit), and will also be questioned and observed as part of an overall prison inspection. This will give rise to an Action Plan of targets and systems that must be in place. In my current role as the Managing Chaplain, I'm the one who is accountable to the governor for whether the team meets all the requirements. These can be as wide-ranging as "ensuring every prisoner who wishes it has access to an hour a week of corporate worship in his registered faith" or as specific as "having a policy for the withdrawal of incense from a prisoner".

It's not something I relish, and it can be hard explaining to generous volunteers, or chaplains who only come into the establishment on a very part-time basis, why I'm nagging them about form-filling and computer records when they just want to get on with what they see as the important stuff. There are one or two who clearly think I'm a hard-hearted bureaucrat, as sometimes I have to say, "No, we can't do that" or "We must refuse that request" – either because it would not be rule-compliant or because there isn't the budget.

Clearly we all have to be very security savvy too – checking gates, carrying personal radios, being aware of the potential for conditioning (an attempt by a prisoner to gradually bring us round to his way of thinking so we then do him some favours). Somehow a chaplain has to be compassionate and receptive, as well as sceptical and cautious.

The foundational legislation for prisons is the Prison Act 1952. Albeit amended and updated several times, it remains in force today and sets out the basics for staffing an establishment. It states that every prison should have a governor, a chaplain, and a medical officer, and "such other officers as may be necessary".

It doesn't always feel as if the chaplain is quite so central or foundational these days, at least not in the eyes of the hierarchy or the budget-setters. There can be quite a divide between the operational staff – that is, the uniformed officers and the governor grades who were once officers – and the non-ops or civilians. Chaplains are classed as civilians, even though we unlock cell doors, face prisoners every day and even supervise small groups by ourselves. On a good day the difference is irrelevant, and all staff work together as a team. On the bad days I've felt like a nuisance, disrespected by staff more than prisoners, and treated as an obstacle to be avoided. It's frustrating. Officers, on the whole, do a brilliant job, largely unseen by the wider world, and in difficult circumstances. But I think partly because of a general decline in religion in society, and partly because of the quasi-military mindset, many officers see chaplains as naïve do-gooders, rather than as fellow professionals, trained to support, challenge, and calm the person in front of them.

This attitude does tend to permeate the higher ranks too. I'm a member of the Senior Management Team (SMT), which collectively is responsible for the day-to-day running of the jail and the well-being of staff and residents alike. Some colleagues on the SMT are hugely supportive and collaborative. I've experienced others in the past who have been patronizing, dismissive, and downright rude about the contribution of chaplains to the task in hand. Of course I've wondered if it's a question of sexism, but I have male chaplain colleagues who report exactly the same treatment. (I'm not sure if I should be pleased about that or not.)

So on the one hand I have a detailed, even pedantic, set of statutory requirements to fulfil, and on the other an almost daily battle for my team to be taken seriously. And that's without the budget restrictions or the tales of woe from the prisoners on the wings!

Sometimes it really does feel as if I'm a long way from being a priest any more. When I do get the chance to get out on the wings, there's usually at least one wag who'll quip, "We thought you'd left, we never see you any more." It's not so funny the thirty-second time, but I suppose they have a point. I *do* "fly a desk" most days now.

My typical day starts somewhere between 7:30 and 8 a.m. when I arrive at the gate. After going through several centrally operated gates to enter the establishment, I'm in my office ten minutes later, and my first thought is caffeine. A quick check of phone messages, my diary and the overnight incidents, then it's on to a series of meetings. These start with a security briefing, then it's the main governor's morning meeting, often followed by another gathering – perhaps to discuss prisoners with complex needs, or possibly Health and Safety. By about 10 a.m., in need of more coffee, it's back to the office to check that all the chaplains are in and to brief them for the day. While they go out on the wings doing the stats, I might write reports, analyse data or check emails. I have to keep an eye on the religious make-up of our prisoner population, and plan chaplain rotas and festivals accordingly. I must also perform management checks on all our systems, making sure we are completing all the relevant forms, keeping appropriate records, and following up requests within the required timescale.

There are HR jobs to do – one-to-one meetings with staff and volunteers, appraisals, training, recruitment, expenses to process. Staff members will come to my office for a chat;

chaplains will look for me to give some guidance. There's rarely time for a lunch break, as that's the time when the team are back in the office, needing a debrief and planning for the afternoon. While they go out on afternoon pastoral visits, or maybe lead a group, I'll often have another meeting – this time maybe about our equality and diversity policy, or what's known as "Safer Custody" – keeping our charges safe from themselves and also reducing violence. Later in the afternoon, around 3:30 or 4 p.m., I'll try to get out on the wings, or I'll tour some of the staff areas. Then it's back to the office, either to prepare for an evening group, or to take advantage of the quieter atmosphere to put some thoughts together for a sermon, or a community talk, or an upcoming series of classes. Unless I'm leaving early to collect the children, or staying late for a group, I'll be in the office until about 6 p.m. The evening may bring a community group talk, possibly some computer-based work, relevant reading, prayers, and then a grateful collapse into bed.

So there is plenty of activity, but not a lot of "religious" work for me. On the other hand, my role could be seen as enabling the rest of my team to get out there and do what they do. I couldn't carry on if I didn't feel we were making a difference somehow. And I know that we are.

Andy was ex-military, inside for GBH following a fight. His girlfriend had dumped him, he didn't see his kids any more, and he'd lost his flat. Things couldn't have been much worse. When one of our chaplains visited him on his first morning he wasn't that interested. Still, he registered himself as "Christian" – one step up from the usual "I'm not really anything: put me down as C of E." He was given a leaflet about our services and that was that. We'd see him around on the wings from time to time. He kept his head down and his military training meant he knuckled down to work. He soon became an "enhanced" worker, allowed a modicum of freedom in his daily routine and he settled into the enhanced wing. But there was nothing to suggest he was really going anywhere in life and gradually he slipped into depression.

Then he met fellow prisoner Jay. Jay was a chapel regular, an exuberant Jamaican, musical, larger than life. He persuaded Andy to come along to the weekly Bible Study held in the chapel – if only for something different to do. We hold three separate evenings of Bible Study, such has been the demand for them. Run by combined teams of qualified chaplains and volunteers from the community, the ninety-minute sessions are a mix of teaching, enquiry, debate, and personal reflection. They're not intended to convert – in fact proselytizing is specifically banned – but for someone curious about faith, or just wanting to ask questions, they're an ideal environment.

Andy came and never looked back. He was an intelligent man and through these sessions he rediscovered the faith of his childhood. He began to attend the weekly Sunday service and before long was reading lessons, encouraging others and facing the demons of his past. He reconnected with his partner, began to see his kids, and contacted his parents. When he was released he immediately began attending a church, has now been baptized and is training for the Christian ministry. Jay is out too, and his music and presentation skills have helped him to set up as a speaker and advocate for faith work in prison.

The influence of other prisoners is often key but equally vital, I believe, is the input from community volunteers. I have a large team of them, and they help with a huge range of tasks. There are trained bereavement counsellors, official prison visitors, pastoral assistants, worship assistants, musicians, group leaders. Often prisoners are amazed when they realize someone is coming in free of charge, just to help them. And what really blows them away is when they hear some of the stories behind it all.

One of my volunteers is an older lady, quite proper in her ways, smartly dressed, and not the sort you'd expect to find helping out in jail. Especially not when you find out her son was killed on a night out some years ago. I recorded an interview with her for a radio show in 2013 and her story was heart-breaking but uplifting at the same time. Seven years earlier, her son had a row with his wife and as a result took himself out into town. In the interview she described his reaction as "going on a rampage, drinking, probably drugs as well". He fell foul of a group of other men and was murdered. She told me about her stunned reaction after having been to identify his body – "I just sat and sat and sat and sat and I couldn't move. I don't know how I slept, I don't know if I slept really, and then I got up in the morning and I just did a whole pile of ironing."

Some while afterwards she heard a person at church speak about visiting in prison. She decided to go herself. When she stood up in front of a group of prisoners to tell the story of her experience, she told me she was suddenly struck with the notion that these men needed help more than castigation. "Who am I to judge?" she thought. And ever since then she has been coming in once a week to help with a small group who study the Bible. She comes because she feels it gives her son's death some meaning. She works with our prisoners to try to divert them away from the lifestyle that killed her son, and that led others to kill him. She believes that hatred and bitterness and prolonged anger don't make things better, don't bring someone back, don't solve the problems. "Locking them up and throwing away the key" is not a constructive attitude, in her mind, nor is it a solution to the waywardness that besets so many of our young men. Hats off to her, and to all the others who come with the same attitude of trying to reach groups of young men whom society doesn't know how to reach.

One of the groups that's causing consternation at present are disaffected young Muslims. Research seems to show that Muslim men are disproportionately represented amongst prisoners, and it's perhaps amongst this group that the Prison Service has had to up its game in the past decade, not least with the provision of chaplains. I participate in regular meetings to assess any prisoners considered either to have extremist views or to be vulnerable to radicalization – in the shadow of atrocities such as the multiple incidents in Paris, this feels like a serious responsibility.

Go back fifteen years or so and there were few chaplains in jail who weren't Christians. Now the teams are fully multi-faith, and it's a requirement of those dreaded regulations that there is a chaplain available every week for the various faiths represented in the population. It's interesting that around two-thirds of all prisoners declare themselves as belonging to one faith or another. After the combined numbers of various Christian denominations, by far the largest group in my jail is the Muslim population. Elsewhere, depending on where the prison is located, it might be the biggest group in that particular jail. So every prison now has at least one Muslim chaplain. They have all the usual responsibilities of pastoral care for their congregation as well as the religious duties of Friday prayers and so on. They also spend a lot of time explaining the truth about their beliefs and practices to staff as it can be a cause of some anxiety for those who aren't familiar with the faith. But Muslim chaplains are also on the frontline of spotting the potential for extremism and diverting people away from it. They will challenge radical views, teaching the mainstream beliefs of their religion, as well as giving personal support to those who might otherwise be vulnerable and fall prey to undue influences. It's quite a burden, particularly as some Muslim prisoners will be very negative towards them as a result – "Government Imam" is one of the more polite insults that's thrown at them.

It's a whole book (or more) in itself, looking at issues of being a Muslim in jail, and not something I'm qualified to talk about except as an observer. It has been good to learn more about this often "demonized" faith. Yes, there are differences and significant points of disagreement. But generally we have been able to explore those together with respect. My Muslim colleagues have, mostly, been generous and gentle people, hospitable, trustworthy, fun, and dedicated. And I have to say that many of the Muslim prisoners I've dealt with have also been grateful for the contact. Still, on the occasions when I have worked with someone convicted for extremism-related offences, I have found it odd how caring and thoughtful they can be towards their own families, whilst seeming to be so callous towards other human beings. But then, that's an observation I can make about most prisoners I encounter – life and other people and their actions are in a series of disconnected boxes. Somehow chaplains must try to work with them to lift the lids of those various boxes and consider the contents in relation to one another.

It's been quite an eye-opener for me, over the years, learning to work alongside colleagues from non-Christian faiths. Growing up in North London I'd had a lot of exposure to Judaism but that was it. These days, as well as leading a team of various Christian flavours, I find myself the boss of two imams, Sikh, Hindu, and Buddhist priests, a rabbi, and a pagan practitioner. I've learned quite a bit about festivals and rituals! Interestingly, only rarely have I had issues with members of the team because I'm a woman. It *has* been difficult for one or two to accept my authority, however gently I exercise it – and I can think of one person I've worked with in the past who was particularly unpleasant. Luckily our paths don't cross these days…

I think mostly those who come to work as prison chaplains are there with the right attitude. We're a team of people with a common goal – to support those in crisis, and to reduce the likelihood of them reoffending. We recognize there are differences between us, but in a stressful, fast-paced environment, the priority is those in our care – religious debates take a back seat and we're more interested in our common humanity than in any quest for superiority. So if I'm the duty chaplain on a given day I'll visit all and everyone, regardless of their badge – as long as they're happy to see me, I'll be there.

It can be incredibly moving to work alongside a chaplain from another faith. In my current jail I have a wonderful Sikh colleague, an elderly, gentle man, who treats me like his grand-daughter. He sponsors an eye hospital for some of the poorest people in India, and he's shown me pictures of the work there, as well as invited me to visit. I have watched his quiet, dignified response to a Sikh prisoner who was berating him for some perceived slight; seen his ministrations to another who was seriously ill; and been delighted when he arrived to support our Christmas carol service.

As another example, I remember a Muslim colleague approaching me in my previous jail, and asking if I'd work with him to care for a particular prisoner. The chap was a

Muslim convert, a regular at Friday prayers, and not someone I knew. His grandmother, who was a Roman Catholic, had just died, and he was not going to be allowed to attend the funeral. So together we brought the prisoner to the multi-faith room, he lit a candle and knelt between us, Muslim chaplain and Christian chaplain. S., the Muslim chaplain, prayed in Arabic, a prayer for the dead. And then I prayed, in English, a Christian prayer of benediction, followed by the "Our Father" prayer. Religious co-operation and mutual respect: it can be done.

I don't "do God" in prison because of some messianic zeal. I don't do it because I need a captive (!) and vulnerable audience for my religious ranting. (I've been accused of all these things – although not by prisoners.) Nor is it to give myself a sense of power, or because I think people are going to hell without religion. We make our own hell, and plenty of men I've met are well-ensconced. I do God, or better put, I encourage spirituality, in jail, because our spirit is an essential part of our humanity. Religion can brutalize us and lead people to do the most terrible things. But faith, spirituality, can also teach us to regard the world and others with respect and wonder. It can show us our own value when experience has told us we're worth nothing. It can give us a focus and a reason for living. It provides examples and role models of a positive kind. Religion can open our eyes to beauty, self-sacrifice, service, and responsibility. Other things can do that too, and I fully recognize that people of no religious faith can be no less altruistic and humane. I don't have a world domination agenda! But the frameworks I understand, the experiences I've had, the encounters I've had with something I can only describe as "other", lead me to couch my work and intentions in spiritual and religious terms.

Once you've come into prison, society has formalized its rejection of you. You've caused hurt and suffering, often unimaginably so, which inevitably diminishes you as a person. The future promises the continued suspicion of others, renewed and repeated rejection, radically affected life chances, maybe even your own ongoing guilt and remorse. The aims of the Prison Service, admirably, are to protect the public, carry out the sentence, and try to assist the individual to lead a law-abiding and productive life in the future: punishment and reform; past and future. Most of my Service colleagues, of all ranks, are trying to achieve these aims. I'm trying to achieve this too, within the framework I've described. My life was turned around by finding faith, and on more than one occasion I don't know how I would have survived without that bigger picture. We don't pay enough attention to the value of hope.

But doing this job in jail is hard and sometimes thankless; frequently it's invisible. Doing it when you don't have enough people, or with ancient equipment, is harder still. There are courses I could put on, or events I could hold, ways I could help and intervene and encourage and inspire – if. If there was a bigger budget, if there were better facilities, if I had more staff and didn't have to rely on those wonderful volunteers for so much. This isn't really a criticism of officials, structures or even government. It's the consequence of society as a whole not wanting to know what happens to criminals after they're locked up. And it's the result of our gradual loss of respect for faith and for the inner person. It can feel as if we're all about image now, about fame and fashion and 140 characters. The mysteries of the soul are too airy-fairy for many and, in any case, religion has hammered several nails into its own coffin.

But I carry on, and so do my colleagues of all faiths up and down the country, because we do see individuals change course, we do see families restored, and we do believe in the power of hope, even for the "vilest offender", to quote a well-known hymn.

From the start of my ministry I've dealt with sex offenders alongside those convicted of crimes ranging from murder to driving without insurance. In the curious hierarchy of the prison world, sex offenders really are the lowest of the low, referred to by other prisoners as "nonces", and they have to be housed separately for their own protection. Even if a prisoner is on remand for a sex offence (not sentenced, not found guilty, and therefore innocent in the eyes of the law) he'd better keep quiet about it. I've known men on remand whose alleged crimes have made it to the papers and they've been subjected immediately to violent threats and verbal abuse.

Increasingly, older men are coming into the prison system, having been convicted of offences that occurred years previously. There are also the younger rapists, the computer-drugged child abusers, and even the occasional shamed clergyman. Sometimes walking onto the sex-offenders (or "vulnerable prisoners") wing is a surreal experience, as you reflect on the level of harm caused by the shuffling figures milling about you. Once or twice a prisoner has made me feel very uncomfortable, and a couple of times a third party has reported to the security team what a prisoner has said he would like to do to me. But I don't usually feel unsafe – most of these men aren't strictly opportunists, and in any case help is only a few steps away.

But working with these prisoners is a huge challenge for me, not least because as a child I was sexually abused over a number of years.

Already a lonely girl, these assaults isolated me further, adding to my sense of shame and self-hatred, my belief that I was worth nothing. I blamed myself for not stopping it of course, even though I had no idea how I could. The actions of this man, combined with other early experiences, crippled my ability to conduct relationships, led to that disastrous behaviour at university, and laid the foundations for the devastating breakdown I suffered in my early 30s.

But it also inadvertently forged in me a strength that still astounds me, and a will to thrive that's helped me to achieve more than I could have ever imagined. After a lot of hard work to deal with the effects of these events, and after many mistakes along the way, I've emerged as someone who *is* capable of love, who loves herself, and is willing to walk with anyone who genuinely wants to face themselves and their actions. A debilitating start does not lead inevitably to a disastrous end.

David was a convicted sex offender. Not a paedophile, not a killer, but "on the rule" nevertheless (Rule 45 of the Prison Rules 1999, allowing for the separate housing of prisoners for their own safety). I first encountered him when I needed some posters making for an event to be held in the chapel, and he was taking part in an IT class. My team tries to get prisoners to do as much of this kind of work as we can – it's constructive; it teaches them skills; it helps them contribute to the community that is the prison. Sometimes this informal work can even help lead to qualifications in IT. David was keen to engage in anything and everything on offer to him in jail – courses, training, and opportunities to understand and reflect on his offending behaviour. He had regular paid work in the prison (it's not exactly a decent salary – only a few quid a week – but the regular work ethic can be helpful, not to say distracting). He also made a point of helping other prisoners, supporting those who were struggling with themselves, the prison rules, the length of their sentence. He did a good job of those posters too.

David will be on the sex offenders' register for life and he knew and accepted that. But he was determined to contribute to society in a positive way, and gained serious qualifications whilst inside to help him to do so. He can't undo what he did and he made a point of addressing the issues of his victim and the effect he had on them. But he can acknowledge his wrongdoing and set off along a different pathway.

I have come to respect that, despite my own experiences. There perhaps are not many like David – I meet plenty more who are in total denial about their crimes (and that's not just the sex offenders). There will always be a proportion who show no remorse, refuse to engage with help, and continue to be a threat to society. As I've described, there are some who seem to be a lost cause. There are those who should never be released. But amongst even the "lowest of the low" there may be a way back up. This is what Paul Jones, father of April Jones, who was murdered by a paedophile in 2012, said in 2015:

"People, they think, 'Why should we help the paedophile? We should be prosecuting them, throwing them in jail, having them castrated.' But if we offer help to paedophiles we might save children who might have been abused."

A controversial view, but one to be heeded, coming as it does from a man whose family has been through such appalling circumstances.

I would want to state quite strongly that I'm no naïve hopeful, oozing tea and sympathy, and I'm not compelled to save the world. Perhaps, after all, I can be hard-hearted sometimes. I meet men who are dangerous, manipulative, violent… drug addicts, abusers, and fraudsters. But I also meet men who are shocked and horrified by their own actions. Or simply bewildered and tired of the life they've lived, wanting to escape it but not knowing how. Some do have a genuine moment of realization, a sudden dawning of the effect they've had on others.

I've always believed justice must be tempered with mercy, law with grace – I'd be a rubbish priest if I didn't. Sister Helen Prejean, the inspiration behind the film *Dead Man Walking* wrote, "People are worth much more than the worst thing they do." I read a blog response to that by an American called C. J. Green, which read: "The worst thing we do stains us, and once people see those stains, it's hard to see beyond them."

That's why I believe the Prison Service continues to need chaplains, even as the budget cuts bite. Not just to be religious functionaries for the various faiths, nor just to apply the rules, tick the boxes, and pass the audits. Chaplains are needed to strike the balance; to see beyond the stains, and to remind the Prison Service, and society, of the need for more than punishment. They are needed to symbolize the wider, deeper aspects of human life – yes, even the "soft" stuff, and to stand for principles such as forgiveness, reparation, co-operation, and hope.

As we work together, across faith and cultural boundaries, bringing profound, sometimes painful, experiences to our daily encounters, what we're doing is modelling how community *can* be, what individuals *can* achieve, and how, even if you're a long way down the road to hell, it's still possible to turn round and head the other way.

CHAPTER 5

FROM HIGH HEELS TO HYMN BOOKS

On a glorious October day in 1987 I married the drummer. The church was filled with Harvest Festival colour, our friends and family, and unbridled hope. Every little girl's fantasy, I'd arrived in a horse and carriage, wearing a Diana-esque dress, and the boys were in top hats and tails. My best friend and a former flatmate were gracious in their willingness to be dressed up in yellow satin, and there was a small relative in a sailor suit. (He's now a dad who drives steam engines in his spare time!)

It was two days after the so-called Great Storm of 1987 and the roads were tree-strewn rather than tree-lined. I'd been staying with friends the few days before and their electricity had been knocked out – I'd had to go up the road to someone else's house to have my hair done and it was touch and go whether there'd be power in the village hall for the reception (there was). Several of the guests had had to endure quite an odyssey to attend, with cancelled trains, blocked roads, and general transport chaos. My maternal family were conspicuous by their absence (out of choice rather than obstacle), but my dad, his parents and my brother were there, and all was well.

Drummer Man and I had got back together after my encounter with the Great Whatever that day in church. Buoyed up with newly discovered evangelical fervour, I gave up karate (having been advised it was A Bad Thing for a Christian woman to pursue) and the illicit substances. We threw ourselves into church life, attending Bible studies and every service going. I cringe to remember how we even subjected the poor vicar to the third degree over his mission to young people, having decided we had a few answers up our sleeves.

There was an older couple that we knew via family – he was an evangelical pastor; she supported him in his role, and found it hard to understand why I might want a separate career. They were most concerned at the danger that Drummer Man and I might give in to carnal urges before we were safely wed, and, young and impressionable as we were, we took their concerns seriously. So just three months after I graduated, and just six months after re-starting our relationship, we were married. I was 21, he was 23, we were in love, and the world was smiling upon us.

My post-university career was not getting off to quite such a splendid start. I'd not really planned on a law degree during my A-level years. I'd wanted to be a set designer and was keen on art school. However, this was not popular with my mother. With hindsight, maybe I wouldn't have been good enough anyway, despite gaining an A for Art A level. Stuck for ideas, I simply copied what my best friend was doing and applied to do law, and with my good grades had no trouble securing a place. Always an amateur dramatist at heart, I decided initially to be a barrister, but it soon became apparent that, lacking contacts and independent means, this was not a road that I could follow. I think there's a part of me that still hankers after the opportunity to mutter "M'learned friend" and "M'lud" but I'm not so sure about the wig... So the alternative was to become a solicitor. Unfortunately in those days one had to apply for a place on the solicitors' training course almost as soon as one arrived in the first lecture, and I'd missed that particular boat. Luckily I'd invited my former head of department to the wedding, and at the reception he asked me what I was going to do for work. On hearing of my dismal failure to get myself organized, he offered me maternity cover as a law tutor.

Now, given my track record as a non-attender at lectures, this was rather a large step of faith – for him as much as me. However I had managed to pull off a decent enough degree and there was now a "wedding loan" to repay, so I had a motivator...

In fact I enjoyed it. I was teaching basic contract law to land management students and I had to give two tutorials a week. It was a huge group – about twenty – and they were not the best-motivated students in the world. At last I was getting my comeuppance: I understood the frustration of the silent stare, or the furtive avoidance of eye-contact, from students who hadn't prepared. One week I even sent them all out of the tutorial and told them to come back next week once they'd done some reading! During that time I also secured a temporary maternity cover contract as a lecturer in law at the local College of Technology. Here I was teaching banking students as well as second-year hopefuls who wanted to become legal executives.

My charges passed their exams (phew!), but the mothers on leave returned, the contracts came to an end, and I was once again casting about for work. I signed up with a temp agency, and found myself packing toys in a factory, assisting a local fledgling computer games company to do their admin, and then answering the phone in a posh voice for a firm of solicitors.

It soon came out that I was a law graduate, and one of the partners at the law firm found out that I hadn't been able to get onto the solicitors' training course in time. Bless him, he rang a former colleague who taught on the course and secured me a place for the following year. In the meantime the firm offered me work as a legal clerk for that intervening year: such kindness.

I spent a year sitting in the firm's subterranean library, filing, researching, updating records (there were few computers back then, so it was all done by hand). For a while I shared a space with a proper articled clerk – together we listened to the news reports from the Lockerbie plane crash while she panicked – she had relatives in the town; thankfully they were fine.

In those days, to qualify as a solicitor you had to attend a full-time, year-long course at one of the four branches of the College of Law, pass the exams, and complete two years as an articled clerk. I decided that the land and property specialism of the firm that had taken me under its wing was not really where my interest lay, as grateful as I was to them. I couldn't see myself as a conveyancing solicitor. Don't forget this was the era of shoulder pads and *LA Law* on TV. I wanted to be a hotshot!

So I secured myself a contract for articles at a different firm, with a reputation for feisty litigation, did a few months with them, and then set off for a year at Guildford College of Law. This meant a daily commute from Reading to Guildford, on a trundling slow train which set off at 7:20 a.m. I lived a thirty-minute walk from the station. At the other end the College was another thirty minutes' walk uphill, and I usually arrived just in time for a 9 a.m. start. Getting home just after 7 p.m., I then had several hours' worth of preparation for the following day. It was a bit of a contrast to my former student experiences.

It was an intense year. We studied a whole range of legal subjects – litigation, divorce, criminal, property, wills – all from a very practical standpoint: "This is the form to fill in when X happens"; "This is how to draft an affidavit"; "This is what a judge will be looking for." I'd always had a good memory and this course certainly tested that. I loved it – such a contrast to the dry delivery of my university days.

I found a good group of friends there, too, and we developed quite a social conscience. It was through them that I had my first experience of prison. HMP Coldingley is not far from Guildford. At the time it was a male Category B prison (it's since changed to a C), in leafy Surrey, near Woking. One of our group was in touch with the chaplain there and we arranged to go in and talk to the prisoners about our experiences in life, to play some music and have a chat. We got together a small band – me on electric guitar, my husband on drums, a bassist, a keyboard player, and a singer. I had a synthesizer at home (a good 1980s instrument!), as well as the guitar, so we agreed to bring both, plus hubby's drums. Our car was a Mini…

Somehow we got an entire drum kit, a guitar, a synth and an amplifier in the back of the Mini. We didn't have a proper stand for the synth, and had been in the habit of using an old ironing board. The ironing board wouldn't fit in the car, so we strapped it on top and off we set. Somewhere along the A329 just outside Bracknell, we became aware of flashing lights behind us, then a burst of blue. Heck. We pulled over and hubs sheepishly wound down the window.

"Good evening, sir," said the bobby, in classic fashion. "Are you aware of the hazard on your roof?"

When we strapped the ironing board to the roof with elasticated ties we hadn't allowed for the laws of aerodynamics. Slipstream plus elastic ties plus large flat thing had resulted in large flat thing standing bolt upright and waving at the world as we drove along… *Mr Bean* had just started appearing on TV back then – this was a perfect echo. Having secured the offending article and avoided a ticket we drove off, not sure whether to giggle or tremble.

We were totally unprepared for what the visit to the jail would be like. Naively we had expected to be able to park close to where we would be setting up. Of course not! Meeting the chaplain at the main gate, and after a thorough search, fifteen students each had to carry a bit of drum kit or amplifier or whatever through numerous gates and up several flights of stairs, all under the bemused gaze of a clutch of uniformed officers. The room we were led into surprised me with how "normal" it looked and felt – a bit like a school classroom. There were pictures and posters on the wall, tea and coffee was set up to one side, and a couple of chaplaincy assistants lurked about. Eventually the prisoners were brought in – a bunch of men in jeans and T-shirts, all looking ordinary.

We played to about twenty prisoners that evening. The student group had decided that I had an interesting personal story so I shared that with the prisoners. Afterwards, over a cup of tea, one of the men came up to me and told me that his story and mine were similar. "If you could get yourself out of it," he pondered, "then maybe I can too. Thank you."

That was a powerful moment for me – I'd never really considered that I might have something in common with a convicted criminal, and I'd certainly never seen "cons" as real people like me before. Yet here I was talking to them. They weren't scary, they didn't have two heads, and some even wanted to lead a different kind of life. I had no leaning towards chaplaincy at that stage – or even towards ordained ministry. I was going to be a lawyer. But as I reflected on the events of the evening, I hoped it would help me to be a more compassionate one.

In fact, I felt there wasn't much scope for compassion once I returned to the feisty law firm. I spent several months shadowing in the insolvency department, and then was let loose on a few cases of my own. This seemed largely to consist of attending County Court hearings around the South of England, applying to declare someone bankrupt and remove their assets, or repossess someone's house after they had defaulted on their mortgage. I was efficiently good at it, but that's not necessarily something to be proud of.

I did enjoy my six months working in the Family Law department. I learned to calm down hysterical clients, became very good at sniffing out when someone was hiding assets from their former spouse, and developed a good line in winning injunctions for battered women. I think one of my proudest moments was when, against a trained and experienced barrister, I won back custody of a woman's children after they had been removed from her because she was suffering from depression. If we think the stigma against mental health is bad now, it was terrible in the 1980s.

The court appearances were the exciting bit for me – that inner barrister trying to come out. I used to love the times when I was sent up to London to the High Court. I'd cross over the pedestrian crossing and walk under the famous Victorian Gothic arches, with my raincoat and briefcase, feeling like I owned the world. Ridiculous of course, and arrogant too, but I was only 23.

Not that it was all easy. I did dread the times when I had to enter the Bear Garden, an area next to the rooms of the Masters of the High Court. A Master is a sort of subset of a judge, largely concerned with procedural matters, and lawyers gather in the Bear Garden and line up to bring issues before the Master as a preliminary to cases being heard in court. In days gone by, papers were lowered down to the waiting lawyers from a gallery above. One day Queen Victoria visited the court and, hearing the noise in this area, she remarked that it sounded like a garden full of bears, and the name stuck. As a young and nervous rookie, it's intimidating to speak before the Master in front of hordes of other lawyers, particularly if you get a grumpy one who shouts at you.

Generally I found the legal world of the time to be a brutal environment, and some of the (male) solicitors I worked with were stereotypical in their hard-drinking, expletive-laden approach to business. It was a sexist world too, and I had to endure personal comments, inappropriate lunges, and patronizing exclusion on a regular basis. Being a hotshot was not all it was cracked up to be.

It only got worse after I found out I was pregnant with my first child in 1990. I was refused time off to go to antenatal classes: my boss declared that if his wife could go to evening sessions, so could I. The fact that the evening sessions were privately run, expensive, and beyond my pocket escaped him. I was hauled before the senior partner and given a grilling as to why I had dared to become pregnant when I was still a trainee. I was removed from any interesting cases and given office work that should have been done by a legal secretary, not a graduate trainee solicitor. Despite my growing bump, I was made to carry heavy bags of documents, chasing after one of the partners at top speed around the streets of London. And at the end of my training contract, I was kicked out without a job.

Thankfully by this stage I was already questioning my future and wondering whether, in fact, my path lay in a different direction. Through my traineeship, I'd met so many people "on the skids" so to speak – financial disasters, marital catastrophes, business collapse – and I'd been turned off by the heartless way we seemed to deal with them, with our powerful corporate clients. I could talk to these people over a desk, maybe win a court case for them, or if I was acting against them, I could be the cause of their downfall. But I wasn't there afterwards to help pick up the pieces, or before to help divert the disaster. It didn't seem enough. I'd met those prisoners, too, and with my husband had continued to visit one of them for a while, as he had no other visitors. There were my own personal experiences in the background. And I had continued to pursue my faith, in a church with a generous and active social conscience. Somehow I wanted to tie all of this together, alongside the creative bits of me that loved to speak, to inspire, to lead. They say the Law, the Church, and the Stage are similar professions – it was time to explore the possibility of becoming a vicar.

I'd been in a taxi on my way to the Law Society in London to collect my certificate of qualification, when the radio announced that the Church of England's General Synod had finally allowed women to become priests. I was delighted for my vicar at home – his wife wanted to join him in ministry but had been blocked thus far, only allowed to be a deacon, the lowest rank of ordained minister. These two were an inspiring couple and they had allowed my husband and me loads of opportunities to lead services and events at the church. So much so that hubby was already on the road to his own ordination.

It took a while to think through what I wanted. By the time I was sure that becoming a priest was the path for me, I'd already left the legal circus, was loving looking after my little girl, and was using my networks and skills to set up and run a Child Contact Centre – one of the early ones in the country, staffed by volunteers, and using the church premises. These facilities are pretty commonplace now but were unusual back then. It was a way of providing a safe and supervised environment for a non-custodial parent to have contact with their child. Most of the time it was dads who waited nervously in our carefully laid out play area, jingling the change in their pockets and clutching the teddy they'd picked up at the shop on the way. The mum would bring the child to a separate entrance, where she could then spend the next couple of hours with a coffee and a sympathetic ear, while the little one was taken through to meet dad for the allotted time. It sounds dreadfully sad, but for most of these families the very fact of arriving at the doors was a huge success in what had been a long and painful journey for all concerned. The courts were, and still are, of the view that, in the absence of abuse or other threat, it is in a child's best interests to have meaningful contact with both parents. Using a Contact Centre was often the first step to normal contact in the future. I remember one father who hadn't seen his kids for 18 months – we were all crying when they stood in the middle of the hall and hugged. I'm really proud that, 23 years on, that Contact Centre is still running.

So at least when I went for "The Chat" with the vicar I had a solid track record on which to base my "I think I should be ordained" claim. He knew me well anyway, and agreed with my notion. The next step was to be referred to the Diocesan Director of Ordinands, or DDO. This was a senior member of the clergy, appointed by the bishop of a particular area, with the responsibility of weeding out the hopeless cases and encouraging the more promising ones. A candidate would meet the DDO over a number of months, often to be set reading and essay-writing tasks, as well as being subjected to some searching interviews. This was to determine whether or not you were bonkers/dangerous/deluded, and also to decide whether you had enough brainpower to cope with the demands of studying obscure theologians for several years. The DDO I met was a lovely chap, and eventually he was convinced enough to refer me on to the bishop, who had the final say about whether or not a candidate should attend a residential selection conference. Boxes? Tick, tick, and tick.

Which is how I found myself turning up at a large but rather shabby convent on the edge of London in the early autumn of 1993. I had just moved to Bristol with hubby, who had himself got through the process at the second attempt, and was starting his training at a residential vicar college. Hubs and I had a vision of sharing a parish sometime in the future, and this was to be the next step. We had a two-year-old and a six-month-old, so it was not the best timing, but I was up for it.

The next two and a half days were a blur of group tests, interviews and written exercises. It was awful. An absolutely horrendous process, where I felt taken to pieces, turned over, and left in bits on the ground. It was clear from the start that my status as a clergy wife was against me, as was the fact that I had two little ones. I found myself defending my wish to have a life other than the purely domestic, and I came away feeling angry, unheard, and more convinced than ever that this was the role for me, even though I knew they would say no.

They did say no.

The person who rang to give me the news stated that ordained couples were a real headache anyway, and suggested I might find fulfilment in supporting my husband in his ministry. This was a red rag to a bull.

Of course, in many ways they were right: I wasn't ready. But not because of motherhood and apple pie. I wasn't ready because I was still all rosy spectacles about the church and its processes. I hadn't grown the rhinoceros skin I would have to develop to survive as a clergyperson. I wasn't ready because, despite my pretty extensive back catalogue of experiences, I still had some more to go through before I could stand by others going through the same.

I didn't see all this at the time, of course. I was simply angry and hurt; all the feelings of rejection I'd managed to bury quite successfully for several years came busting out all over. And to cap it all, I was smack bang in the middle of a bunch of people all studying for the very thing I ached to do. I'd see hubs off to college every morning, faced with the knowledge that I was on the outside of it all. Of course I resented it and I resented him. It wasn't his fault, but he symbolized all that I saw as sexist and unfeeling and uncaring about the church.

I loved my kids to bits, but I couldn't understand why it was OK for a man to have small children and pursue his dream, but not a woman. Same old story.

The bishop from back home was lovely. I went to see him and he was gentle and kind and encouraging. He's dead now, but of all the bishops I've met, he seemed to me to be the holiest and wisest. He told me that he was tempted to overturn the decision (he had the power to do so) but that he thought it would undermine my eventual success (which he was convinced would come). So he gave me some money, as did the lovely people of my home church, and told me to study what I could under my own steam, and return to a selection conference in two years' time. At least I felt there were some people who believed in me! So I enrolled and paid for part-time study, alongside the bona fide students, reading the obscure theologians and crafting the essays late into the night around toddler groups, chickenpox, and visits to the zoo.

It came for all the wrong reasons, but that difficult, demanding time was good for me. It really did test my resolve. How much did I want this? I wanted it. And not just because I'd been thwarted once, although I did have to examine that as a motivation very carefully indeed. The old bloody-mindedness again. I wanted it because, naff as it may sound, deep down I knew this was what I should be doing with my life.

My history of damage and rejection and confusion, and my working life to date, coupled with the mysterious comfort and purpose I gained from that strange experience in church, had convinced me that I could talk to people about a way out of the depths. I was of the view, and still am in some ways, that the Church doesn't reach people because too often it occupies a space so far removed from messy real life. *My* real life was very messy and was going to get messier. If I could use that to shine a bit of light somewhere then I wholeheartedly wanted to. It was as if that's what I was born to do. I guess that's what you would call a vocation, and I think it's been put to good use in the prisons.

Prisons *are* dark places, often literally as well as figuratively. HMP Bedford is an old Victorian jail, with small windows and little corridors. My current office barely admits any daylight. I can leave in the evening with no idea whatsoever what the weather has been like all day. But prisons can be places of incredible humanity too. By this I mean all the pretence is stripped away. Men still strut about on the wings, still play a very dangerous game with one another, still manipulate and terrorize and attack. There's all the Mr Big role-play you might expect, and plenty of guys who are so buried in their own self-justification they're unable to recognize when someone is genuinely trying to help. But really, there's no more pretending that life is OK once you're inside. Once you accept that, facing up to yourself, as scary as that might be, can no longer be ignored.

And if you're prepared to accept it there's a lot of help. It's true that lower staff numbers, tight budgets, and short sentences make formal interventions very difficult to deliver. It's true that someone's life chances after prison are often worse than when they went in. But it's also true that most prison staff will treat offenders with humour and decency, especially if that offender is trying to make a go of things. I've known officers who will give their all to support and encourage someone trying to go straight. I've seen them desperately try to save a prisoner's life and weep when they fail. I've seen them demonstrate patience and empathy and wisdom, and I've learned a huge amount from them.

As well as some dreadful language...

As time has gone on I've quite clearly not been what you might call the typical vicar. Good. I've wanted to show people that you can be ordinary, you can mess things up, you can make mistakes, stumble and get up again, enjoy a bit of craziness – and still have faith in something mysterious and holy and a little bit wild, that some people call "God". I don't believe that spirituality requires perfection. In truth, neither do most of my clergy colleagues, but perhaps, for some, their take on imperfection is a bit neater than mine.

There was plenty of imperfection during those vicar school years and my marriage really struggled. Not just because of the clergy thing, although that really didn't help. Small kids, lack of money, tiredness, little family support – all the usual candidates causing creeping disillusion and distance. His character, my character, his weaknesses, mine: by the time I was ready for the next selection conference, he was almost at the end of his training period, and we'd already discussed splitting up.

I got through the second time. It was a completely different experience, almost fun. We were gathered at another convent, this time in newly trendy East London. I'd spent the night before D-day staying with my best friend who lived nearby, so had prepared with a decent red and a cigar (we've had some crazy times together). The format was pretty much the same – group exercises, interviews, and written submissions. In one of the group exercises we had to sit in a circle and write a random subject on a piece of paper. The papers went into a bowl and then one by one we drew one out. We had to speak for a minute on whatever subject was written on the paper, then chair a discussion on said subject for three minutes, before summing up in a final minute. I got "transport" (thank you, God!). Meanwhile the examiners were sitting outside the circle writing notes. Apart from the adrenalin when it came to your turn, it was interesting observing the different approaches. Some candidates did what they could to help others during the discussion; others were competitive and tried to make their colleagues look silly. I never knew which ones got through.

The written test took the form of writing a pastoral letter to someone who had approached you with a knotty problem. We were supposed to avoid the urge to write, "Oh, for goodness' sake" to the fictional congregation member, and instead offer delicately balanced encouragement and wise insight. Judging by my fellow clergy Facebook feeds these days, most of us have spent the decades since our ordination pretty consistently thinking, "Oh, for goodness' sake!"

It became obvious that even the mealtimes were a subtle form of assessment. How did you mingle, were you overbearing, could you relate to different ages and backgrounds? Then there were three interviews, looking at your academic aptitude, your spiritual maturity, and your personal life. After two and a half days I emerged exhausted but with a quiet sense of confidence. I'd have to wait nearly three weeks for the verdict, but something told me it would be OK.

I think I had proven myself and maybe I'd learned the system a bit better too – I knew what the panel was looking for. It wasn't a case of just saying what they wanted to hear – that would have been mad, because ordained life isn't for the faint-hearted – but perhaps it was a case of knowing how to represent myself in a way that didn't have them running for the hills. When the call came I was delighted. Delighted, relieved, vindicated.

I now had the official go-ahead from the Church of England, but I still had to do more training, or "formation". My three years as a part-timer got me halfway through the required qualification. I was a graduate over thirty, so didn't need a second degree, but I did need a Diploma in Theology. This I acquired through another two years of part-time study, by now a dab hand at midnight essay writing. I added part-time employment into the mix as well – ranging from a stint in Woolworth's, to legal adviser for a credit control company, to working for the local Highways Department, overseeing their band of School Crossing Patrol Officers (lollipop ladies to you and me).

The kids started school; my training was nearly over. We were by now living in a small market town, where my husband was a curate (a bit like an articled clerk, but in vicar-land). It should have been the sweetest time, as we got ready for being curates together and fulfilling what we'd both worked so hard for. We had spent the past few years trying very hard to keep our relationship going, but we were failing miserably – or should I say spectacularly. We began to alternate between turning on each other and retreating into ourselves. Even the counselling we went for seemed to no avail, and life was pretty sad.

I shouldn't have been surprised when my husband said he was leaving. I shouldn't have been shocked, terrified, thrown into a howling mixture of anger and misery. I'd seen it coming. But I'd closed my eyes, hung on, thinking it would all work out somehow, relying on our shared history, the battles we'd fought together, the love we had for our kids. In March 1998, three months before I was due to be ordained, my life really did fall apart.

CHAPTER 6

LOSING THE PLOT

On "seg round" duty one day, I looked through a small hatch into a darkened cell. With only a dim light filtering through the high, barred window, I could barely make out the shape of a man hunched on the bed. Although I normally carry a cell key, I'm not allowed to open cell doors on the segregation unit. In any case the doors can't be unlocked unless there are two members of uniformed staff present – sometimes three if a prisoner's risk assessment requires it. There was only one around this particular day, so unless I could come back later, I was not going to be able to hold a conversation with this prisoner face to face. I'd have to do my best through the glass of the hatch (observation panel), maybe speaking close to the crack between the heavy steel cell door and the wall. In situations like this I still needed to speak to the guy, check he was alive, as OK as he could be, find out if there was anything he needed or wanted to ask. Segregation is an unpleasant experience – of course – and we have to be more vigilant than usual in ensuring the basic safety and welfare of a prisoner held thus.

I looked down briefly at the notes I held in my hand – occupant's name, prison number – when *bang!* In a second he had leapt up off the bed, bounded across the few feet of floor space, and smashed his hand against the observation panel. Wild eyes, lank hair, lips stretched in… what? Anger? Despair?

I wasn't scared. He couldn't get to me through the thick steel. I was startled though. I knew he'd been brought to the seg cell, down in the gloomy basement, because he'd threatened another prisoner with a home-made weapon, a shank, which is a blade or sharpened bit of metal, either attached to a crude handle, perhaps a toothbrush or a plastic knife, or just wrapped in cloth. But in that brief moment he'd seemed so… undone.

After his outburst Viktor sunk back onto the rumpled bed, head in hands, and I could get nothing more out of him.

Chaplains visit the seg unit every day, visiting men who have been placed on their own because of violence, or persistent extreme behaviour. For a week none of the various chaplains who went to Viktor's door, nor the unit staff who looked after him hour after hour, could get him to engage. Like all segregated prisoners, Viktor was visited by a doctor and the duty governor every day. He sat in his cell, silent, occasionally looking up with such hardness in his eyes that he seemed beyond all human help. He wouldn't shower, wouldn't eat. A foul smell began to emanate from his cell, but he was too dangerous even for a fellow prisoner (known as an orderly) to be allowed to go into his cell to clean it up.

A week later he was brought before the duty governor for another review of what would happen to him. I sat in on this semi-formal meeting, along with a member of the Independent Monitoring Board (does exactly what it says on the tin), a mental health nurse, and three officers. Viktor was Eastern European, so, to ensure he understood what was happening, and in another attempt to get through to him, we had made use of the language line. This was a system whereby we telephoned a number and were then hooked up with an interpreter, so we were able to conduct a three-way conference call between ourselves, the prisoner, and the interpreter.

Viktor broke his silence that morning but the words he spoke were so confused, so disconnected, and the ideas he expressed so outlandish and paranoid, that even the interpreter gave up in the end. Viktor began to get more aggressive and he was ushered back to the darkness of his cell (thankfully the orderly had managed to nip in and clean it up a bit). To a layperson Viktor struck me as mentally ill but the nurse couldn't make that diagnosis without a proper assessment – which was almost impossible to conduct because of the way he presented.

This went on for weeks. Occasionally he would speak to me, or another chaplain, and we managed to piece together a story about family back home, threats from gangs there, weapons, and Viktor's utter conviction that he was going to die. We couldn't work out whether he meant by his own hand, and therefore that he was a suicide risk, or whether he meant someone was going to kill him – in jail or elsewhere. It was so very hard to help him, or even understand what was behind his aggression and violence. He was placed into the system of extra care and observation the Prison Service uses when a prisoner's safety and well-being may be at risk and his incarceration in the seg unit was reviewed regularly. But it was impossible to put him anywhere else; he was prone to such violent outbursts.

Viktor continued to lose weight, continued to ramble, and the only way I can describe his state was feral. Staff did all they could to help him, but the situation was untenable, and he was getting worse. Eventually, after huge amounts of effort from officers, governors and the mental health team, a place was found for Viktor at a secure mental hospital, where he would be sectioned and undergo assessment and treatment.

It was dreadful, watching someone disintegrate so comprehensively. Thankfully I haven't seen such extremes too often, although Viktor's case isn't unique. Sometimes a man's mental health deteriorates quickly as a result of the shock of what he has done. I remember another young man who didn't speak for six weeks after being remanded in custody for a double murder. Then there are others who have struggled with mental health problems for years, often linked to alcohol and drug misuse. Their chaotic life and violent responses are an outworking of their mental ill-health, and their inability to cope with everyday challenges. Others are depressed, or anxious, some have personality disorders (not strictly a mental illness as they can't be treated, but debilitating and life-limiting all the same). The mental health team has to be one of the busiest in the jail.

Every morning the senior staff (governors, senior uniformed officers, medics, chaplain) get together for the morning meeting. This is a kind of summary of the previous day, a briefing for the day to come and a chance to share any immediate concerns. There are usually about twenty of us around the table. I often note the deadpan way in which the "smash ups", the misbehaviour, and the self-harm are reported; factual, low-key, sometimes even bleakly humorous. Every profession has its black humour. Parish clergy usually have tales of funeral faux-pas. Broadcasters recall swear-words slipping out live – I remember making a dirty joke on air by mistake. And in prison we sometimes have to josh about sad and difficult situations – it's how to stay sane ourselves.

It's not that we don't care – we do, otherwise we wouldn't stick to the job – but it's all so familiar, so regular. You can't get emotional about it. For a start, that would be unprofessional and could lead to inappropriate decision-making. But more than that, it would so quickly become overwhelming.

Even some of the prisoners describe *themselves* as mad as a box of frogs, and I can think of one who would regularly laugh at himself and his manic phases. Staff became very fond of Bob, whose brain was addled by drink, but who could be good-humoured and at times hysterically funny. He was another example of that humanity I've mentioned, when it's obvious that someone is completely incapable of life "on the out", and for whom prison staff become a kind of family.

There are lots of structures in place to diagnose, treat, and support prisoners with mental health problems, but inevitably jail isn't the place for someone to find respite and tender loving care. When I walk onto the wings I'm still sometimes struck by the noise, the smell, the testosterone-fuelled tension that comes with hundreds of men locked up together. There really is nowhere to find peace and quiet – except maybe the chapel.

When we can, we'll bring a prisoner to the chapel, which in my current jail is on the top floor of the oldest part of the building. Here he can light a candle in memory of a loved one, have a cry, talk to one of us about what's happening. Occasionally we can arrange for his own community minister to come in and visit, maintaining a vital link with home. We're always keeping an eye on what's going to happen to someone after his release, and if there are any ties we can strengthen, then so much the better. If a man feels he has a stake in a community somewhere, if he can even glimpse a notion of belonging, then his chances of rehabilitation are improved.

Along with other Christian colleagues, I lead services on a Sunday. When it's my turn on the rota I always try to factor in some quiet moments: at the beginning maybe, to bring to mind loved ones who have died; or after the reading or sermon, just to give men an opportunity to reflect and savour the peace. It drops with a tangible weight, that quiet, and is a precious thing.

Sometimes peace and quiet is the last thing a man needs. It's often noisy at night as well as during the day in the prison, but when it does go quiet, prisoners tell me they can find that even more oppressive. In the long stretches of the night there's too much time to think, and worries about family, the future, and the consequences of guilt can weigh heavily.

When I give a talk to a community group, I often ask them to think back to a time in their life, whether as a child or adult, when they did something wrong. This usually produces some uncomfortable shuffling and a few wry smiles, and I think I could probably put money on the likelihood of most of them recalling a childhood misdemeanour. Once a (private) example has been identified, I then ask for single words to describe the feelings evoked. We get shame, guilt, and embarrassment. With the more obvious words out of the way, and as people really begin to relive the experience, many will realize that one of the things they felt was isolation. Their wrongdoing sealed them in a guilty bubble – they couldn't tell anyone, they knew something no one else did, and it affected their relationships. When they were found out, the isolation often increased, as punishment was served. Later, the sense of relief at being forgiven, at being admitted once again back into the fold was palpable.

This isolation, being cut off, is one of the central tenets of Christian theology, and I suspect would not be dismissed by much psychological theory either. Wrongdoing isolates us from family, community, peers, and self. If you add into this mix people who, from an early age, have a sense of detachment from society – through poverty, educational failure, mental illness or simply absorbed rhetoric – then the scale of the task of rehabilitation becomes apparent.

Thus isolated, many men turn inwards and become lost in a mist of depression. Unable to articulate feelings of rage, frustration, and fear, self-harm becomes the vehicle of expression. Sometimes this takes the form of head-banging, occasionally ligature-tying, but most often the method of choice is cutting. Arms, legs, torso; razor blades, sharpened plastic cutlery, sometimes the tiniest bit of metal. Some of the scars are terrible to behold, others are just superficial scratches, but it's all part of the same spectrum – a physical, external expression of an internal and overwhelming emotion – a kind of sacrament of distress.

It is sadly true that some will use self-harm as manipulation – "If you don't give me what I want I'll cut/jump off the top floor/hang myself" – but even that is a symptom of someone's inability to express their needs in a coherent way. It would be very easy for those of us working in jails to become complacent about self-harm, especially amongst those we see using it to coerce. "Him again," a shrug, and move on to the next one on the list. But despite the frustration, the déjà vu, even the anger it provokes in us, we must take each incident seriously, even if it's only to confront a man about his pattern of behaviour. Because the last thing any of us wants is to hear the call over the radio: "Urgent assistance required, Code Blue."

This means that someone appears to be unconscious, not breathing, possibly dead.

Because I carry a cell key, there's always the possibility that I'll open a door one day and find someone in such a state. Thankfully, thus far, I have not been first on scene. I do know from the colleagues I've supported that it is one of the most distressing experiences for an officer, although often the enormity of it doesn't hit till later. Confronted with someone who may be in a life-threatening state, the training kicks in. There's a well-rehearsed, well-orchestrated set of procedures for such an incident. No one wants it to happen, everyone does actually work very hard to try to ensure it doesn't (despite what some press reports might suggest), but we'd be crazy not to plan for it.

Part of that plan is for the chaplain to be called as soon as possible. If a person is close to death, there are many religions which require a version of the last rites. After death, too, there are often prayers needed. It's a delicate operation though, as any evidence at the scene has to be preserved, so the chaplain must touch as little as possible, and get out of the way as soon as the religious duties are done. The police and paramedics will be called, eventually the body removed, and the cell sealed for investigation. And the family has to be informed.

I've done this several times – too many times. The prison will appoint a Family Liaison Officer, or FLO – someone trained and well-suited for linking with a bereaved family. Sometimes that's the chaplain, not always. I prefer to retain a distinctive pastoral and spiritual presence rather than get drawn into the procedure and practicalities of the aftermath, so I have chosen not to be an FLO. In any case a chaplain will always go with the FLO to a family home to break the news of a death, whatever time of day or night it is. We're going to an unknown situation so need to take police advice on any previously reported issues at the address. We take a taxi and ask the taxi to wait for however long it takes. There's certainly no rush.

Sometimes the news is a veritable bomb under someone's life. Other times, possibly more often, it's a horrible shock but not entirely unexpected. Now and again it seems to come as a sad relief.

There's a way to break bad news to someone – something for which we are trained, much as medics and police officers are. Introduce yourself, try to get the person to sit down. Then give them a shot across the bows – a verbal warning that something bad is coming – perhaps, "You must be wondering why I'm here. I'm afraid I have some very bad news for you." And then be clear, concise, and direct: "I'm sorry to have to tell you that X has died." That clarity is hugely important because at times of shock we tend to shut down, and will filter out extraneous words and noises. It's important that the recipient of the news understands in simple terms what has happened. Give brief, honest information, and express sympathy. Don't leave them by themselves, let them know what will happen next, and tell them when you will next be in touch.

Although the family is the first priority, my team will also mobilize to support the staff, who themselves may well be in shock. And there needs to be follow up with other prisoners, especially if there was someone sharing the cell, a padmate. Padmates can be wonderful at supporting each other, making staff aware of concerns, and helping each other through the darkest hours, but the sense of guilt and failure that can grip a padmate who didn't wake up in time can be devastating.

In time a chaplain may well lead a memorial service in the prison (possibly even the funeral). Later, there'll be an inquest, searching questions asked, more staff to support (not least the governor), and a review of all our procedures and training. The loss of a life is far more significant than the paperwork afterwards, but the ramifications of a death in custody run far and wide.

One of the things that has struck me about mental illness and emotional distress in prison is that it's far more acceptable than in wider circles. Sadly, we in polite society do tend to equate mental illness with being a junkie or a criminal, or being born on a sink estate, and sufferers can be ostracized and abused. From what I've seen I don't believe the medical *treatment* of prisoners is any better than it is for others – possibly quite the opposite, given the sheer scale of numbers, and pressures on a diminishing number of mental health professionals working in a custodial setting. There are clearly some who are in custody who would be far better served with a hospital place instead. But there isn't the same degree of stigma attached to mental ill-health by the inside community as there is by those on the outside. Maybe it's familiarity (a sad indictment in itself) or maybe both staff and prisoners are operating at the sharp end of human life, and have more understanding of the pressures that lead to times of imbalance.

Outside, in normal society, we still have a long way to go before the stigma of mental illness is thrown to the four winds. There remains an instinctive reaction that means a sufferer is regarded with suspicion, even though I do believe responses have improved, thanks to recent high-profile campaigns. When I began to unravel in the late 1990s, I soon found out how cruel that stigma could be.

I was 32, with two kids under eight and my ordination looming, I had exams to get through and my marriage was in tatters. Because of the very public nature of our roles in the local community, everybody had an opinion. As my husband was a curate in the local church – young, creative, interesting – many commentators deemed the break-up must be all my fault. One person's first reaction upon hearing the news from my devastated lips was, "What a disaster for the parish."

Despite the whispers, I just ploughed on at first. Those exams had to be passed, the school run didn't go away, and I had to make sure I was financially stable. People began to utter approval: "Oh, you're doing so well." I went on holiday and when I came back there was a presumption that I'd just get on with life. Just a few short months after the drama of the split, someone remarked, "You just need to put it behind you."

A decade later, in 2009, I was invited to write a script for a Radio 4 programme on World Mental Health Day. As part of that I wrote about the big black hole that felt like it was opening up inside me, threatening to swallow me whole. The trouble was, as I was experiencing this growing despair, nobody really wanted to hear about it. I think it was easier for people to assume I was doing OK because I did just try to carry on. And the general view people have of the clergy is that we simply place everything in God's hands and cheerfully get on with it.

After a few weeks of feeling dreadful I summoned the courage to go to the doctor. It's as if the flood-gates opened: I sat in the surgery and sobbed. I could no longer avoid the truth that I felt utterly worthless. In this wretched state I was too bewildered to pretend everything was normal any more.

So I collapsed in on myself. Diagnosed with clinical depression, I was prescribed medication and allocated a Community Psychiatric Nurse (CPN). But my symptoms became worse and eventually I made a serious attempt to kill myself. This was too much for many who knew me – the sympathy evaporated.

I'd been really grateful for those who had called by the house or offered help with the ironing or shopping. But those offers dried up. People who met me in the street didn't know what to say – they were uncomfortable and embarrassed. Some became very judgmental and disapproving – one person shouted at me, angry at my weakness, when as a "baby vicar" I should have been strong. My downward trajectory was a challenge to the ordered predictability most people prefer. I admit, my behaviour could be odd. Befuddled by medication I might set off for a walk, but be so "elsewhere" that I'd find myself coming to, hours later, still walking. I was in a kind of stupor, and would often feel detached and unreal.

I spent about a year and a half in this state. During that time I was admitted to hospital numerous times, I began self-harming, and took an overdose of tablets more than once. I felt completely alone – but the reaction I received from others most often was a mixture of suspicion and fear.

It's the same reaction many people receive once they've been in jail.

I don't think I have ever been as frightened as I was during my time in a psychiatric hospital. The day I was first sent, as a voluntary patient, my home was suddenly taken over by strangers. I'd been seeing the doctor for a while, taking anti-depressants which seemed to do nothing, had been losing weight steadily as I punished myself by starvation. I'd already had an overnight stay in A and E a few weeks earlier, after an overdose of paracetamol. That day, I just lost my tentative grip. I cut my arms – not a suicide attempt, but an expression of anguish. Unfortunately the doc came round while the knife was still in my hands. Poor man, he must have thought I was going to get him next! Nothing was further from my mind. It was me who the world didn't need any more.

But of course the whole machinery kicked in. The children came home from school and were whisked off to relatives, a CPN kept me under constant surveillance as I lay on the sofa in a daze, the doctor paced around, talking on the phone, trying to find me a bed. Then the ambulance came, the neighbours twitched their curtains, and I was half-carried out of the door and driven away. I had no personal items, no bag, no one with me and no idea where I was being taken. When we arrived at the hospital I was gripped on either side by a burly bloke, which was horrific. I remember bucking and pulling, only to be gripped tighter. Bundled upstairs and left in a small room, I curled up into a tight little ball on the bed and shut my eyes, shut out the fear and disorientation. After I don't know how long, someone came and fired questions at me, impatient when I wouldn't (couldn't!) answer. For the next 48 hours I was on constant watch – and that means literally constant, every move under someone's gaze. Oh, the humiliation of using the lavatory, or taking a shower, with a complete stranger watching. Naked in body, mind, and spirit.

I spent eleven weeks in hospital that first time, first in a private facility, and then I was moved to an NHS establishment nearer home. Think *One Flew Over the Cuckoo's Nest* and you're not far off. Things may have moved on in the years that have followed, but back then, there was the shame of being ejected from bed, still in pyjamas, to stand in line to receive medication, and being made to prove that I'd swallowed it. I was lying in bed one night, and the curtains were ripped open violently by a fellow patient, clearly having an episode, who just screamed obscenities at me before being dragged away, howling. Then there was the male nurse who made sexual advances to me. There were case reviews, where I was ushered into a room full of people, none of whom I knew, and expected to spill the most intimate details of my life. All privacy and dignity was shattered. It wasn't treatment; it was a holding place. Was it any wonder I made out I was better than I was, simply to get out?

Which is why, a few months later, I was as bad as ever again. I had stopped taking my medication, hating my dependence on it, wanting to regain control of my life, not realizing the effect it would have on me if I stopped. The depression returned, I couldn't do my job, there was ongoing conflict over what was now a divorce, and during the course of conversations with the CPN, some of the other trauma from earlier years began to come out. The trouble is, once that particular genie gets out of the lamp, it doesn't go back in again after a session of 50 minutes. So I began to deal with my distress by self-harming again. I'd cut my arms with a razor blade. It amazes me now how I felt almost nothing when I did it, not physically anyway, and could slash away at my skin, watching as the blood began to flow. Emotionally there was a degree of relief and release – inner pain on the outside for a bit. Unfortunately this was misunderstood and taken as a suicide attempt each time. Eventually I was bundled back to hospital again.

I so did not want to be there. I didn't want to be apart from my children. I didn't want to breathe in the horrible, fetid, oppressive atmosphere of the place. I tried to leave – and was promptly sectioned for 28 days and placed on a locked ward. I was, in effect, in custody.

So when a newly remanded prisoner looks at me with that panic in his eyes, I know. To some degree, I know what it's like to be shamed and rejected. I know what it's like to lose all control over your life. And I know what it's like to be on the wrong side of a locked door, with no way out.

My shame was complete when one of the social workers called in to verify the grounds for my sectioning turned out to be a woman who had trained on the same ordination course as me. She was professional, kind, but my descent seemed somehow total after she walked in. I was to be detained for a month for the purpose of assessment. If I was deemed to be enough of a risk to myself or others, I could be sectioned for a further six months at the end of the 28 days – it was serious.

In that Radio 4 programme I described my emotions thus:

"It was like a never ending winter, with trees stripped bare, leaving only a stark silhouette against a cold, white sky. The whole world in shades of grey – all colour and life drained away. Except for the flashes of fear and paranoia, the gut-twisting, heart-hammering moments when the scenery around me, wherever I might be, would fill with a sense of dread so palpable it seemed to take on solid form."

I tried to talk about my childhood, the abuse, the confusion I had felt my whole life, the desperation of having lost the one thing that had given me stability – my marriage. Years later I could see how much I had contributed to the demise of that relationship – I was a difficult person to be with, my deep insecurities at times rendering me irrational, demanding, and impulsive. But that realization only came with maturity and reflection – at the time all I could sense was loss, loss, and more loss.

But no matter how I tried to talk about these things, nobody was listening. Nurses didn't have the time and to the psychiatrist I was just another depressed woman. I wrote poetry to attempt some self-expression, but the doc just told me it was rather heavy and obscure. My boss came to see me, but was at a loss. His boss came too, but all I felt from him was disapproval. A family member became a cliché, and told me to snap out of it. Thus further isolated, I felt I had been taken away from the world. I was no longer necessary, I had no voice, no reason for existing. And yes, I had the conviction at times that I was better off dead.

It was a surreal month. There were only two of us in closed conditions, with two nurses at all times. A small grassed courtyard with a high fence was our only access to the outside. There were a few tatty books, and 24-hour TV. No activities, very limited visits. I'm not sure how it was supposed to make me feel better. Maybe the sheer boredom was designed to subdue the restless spirit.

I was medicated with yet another type of anti-depressant and anti-psychotics too. Enforced inactivity together with supervised meals meant I put weight back on. Generally I became compliant, quiet – most unlike me! Except for one memorable occasion, on Easter Saturday 1999, when I became so frustrated about being cooped up that I threw a chair across the room. All hell broke loose. Alarm bells went off, staff came running, I was restrained and bundled onto a nearby sofa, where I was pinned down by two nurses. I hadn't hurt anyone, hadn't broken anything – but that was it. I was banned from my visit the following day and confined in my room.

This made me so angry that I became determined that this was not going to be my future. From then on I made an effort to dress, to converse, to engage. Weeks later my psychiatrist told me I had been within a hair's breadth of forcible ECT, but that my change in demeanour after that Easter weekend had rendered it unnecessary. Resurrection indeed! At the end of the 28 days I returned to the main ward, and within another month was home. There was still a long way to go, and a few more brief stays in hospital, but I never hit such a low again.

People have asked me since, "But what about your kids? Didn't they give you a reason for being?" Rationally, of course they did. Poor little things, they were only seven and five when their dad and I split up, and the 18 months of my disintegration were a nightmare for them. When they were with me I was much better. Their needs, their routines – I always kept these going. They were fed, clothed, taken to school. We even laughed and had fun. No medic or social worker ever deemed them to be at risk – and you can be sure they checked. My son and daughter tell me they always knew they were loved. But when they went to their father's, away for a long weekend, or a week, the world would collapse again, and this is when I usually turned in on my personal drama, unable to sustain myself. I have felt guilty ever since about the things they had to go through – being whisked off at the last minute, coming to see me in hospital for an hour a week, long journeys to school from their dad's house, the confusion they endured. I see in them still the effects of that time, although we have had many a conversation about it, and they have grown into wonderful adults, to whom I am very close. I was just so engulfed by the power of the forces within.

I can understand why he did it now, but when, in the summer of 1999, my ex-husband served me with a court application for full custody of the children, not only did I hate him, but my mother tiger instinct kicked in. It was the saving of me.

There were a handful of people who understood, who could still see the real me underneath the mayhem, and who supported me through the custody case. Most did not, including some close family members, and they haven't spoken to me since. I really did find out who was my friend in need that June and July. How ironic was it – the former lawyer, who'd enjoyed helping others get their kids back, now fighting for her own in a family court?

It's as if so many of my experiences have almost been designed to get me to see life from the other side of the fence. To understand the underdog, you have to become the underdog. No person's experience is the same as another's, and I would never dare to say to someone, "I know how you feel." I don't. But I might have some idea. It gives what I do an authenticity. I'm not just a middle-class do-gooder; I have actually been there. It was hell at the time. In fact, taken as a whole, it was years of hell. But those years have now become a gift. They're an amazing resource for my work as a priest, especially in prison. And having come so close to losing everything that mattered, I now value what I have so much more.

So I sat in the District Judge's room, a solicitor and barrister by my side (thank God for Legal Aid – I wouldn't get it now). Across the table, was the man I had once loved with all my (faulty) heart, the quirky, geeky, clever drummer. Now we were opposing parties, the saddest of endings. The judge ordered in my favour; the children were to return home.

As I fell into the arms of my best friend who had waited for me outside, I vowed to wean myself off the medication once and for all and get my life in order.

Gradually stability returned. I would wake up able to face life, able to receive each day as a gift of potential. I've described it as feeling as if I were windswept, the way you do when you come into a warm house after braving a raging storm outside. There's no doubt I had been taken to pieces by my experience but now it felt as if I were being put back together again, but in a new and wiser way.

I had to accept that things were changed completely – my old life was gone. But I was still ordained and still had that urge in me to share my understanding of faith and the inner spirit. I could do that now from a very different perspective, from having known, and survived, tremendous weakness and vulnerability.

I often think back to those days when illness engulfed me. I remember the small kindnesses that people showed me, the little flashes of humanity when I felt imprisoned in the dark. I still have the gift one colleague brought me – a small wooden cross, shaped to fit in my hand. She urged me simply to hold onto it, to cling to this reminder of her care, and my faith, when the prayers wouldn't come. To this day I have the silky gold wrap given to me by a fellow patient – given for no other reason than that I said I liked it when I saw her wearing it.

I know I felt alone, but looking back there were those blessed ones who didn't turn away or leave me. The hospital chaplain who visited regularly; the dear friends who stuck by me; the unshakeable, undeserved love of my kids, who forgave me everything. And my dad – cuddly, calm Dad, who proved that blood doesn't make you family; loyalty does. He never judged me, never criticized me, never backed away. They may not have had wings, but these were my ministering angels – and through them I believe God held onto me.

It's still a bit tricky, sometimes, having a colourful medical record, even though it was years ago. Life insurance was hard to get for a while, and more expensive. Every job application has brought with it an intrusive scrutiny into my current mental state (it's been strong ever since). There's still the possibility that if I'm called as a legal witness, or perhaps if I make a formal protest about something, I'll be labelled and disregarded as someone with a history of mental illness. In fact, I discovered only recently that GP surgeries hold a register of people with mental health issues – your name can be on it without your knowledge. I found this out because I changed GP and was sent a letter informing me that, because I had a history of psychological problems, I was to be invited for a general health review every year. Puzzled and somewhat disconcerted, I rang the practice. My previous GP had assigned me to the register all those years ago, and even though they had since put "in full remission" on my notes at every annual review since, they had never told me, never called me in for a discussion, and never removed my name. So when the notes were passed over to the new doctor, they simply received a computer code telling them I had ongoing mental health issues. One robust conversation later and my name has been removed...

But despite all this I'm happy to add my voice to those who are unashamed about their struggles. If my story can help someone else then it has meaning and grace. I hope that my openness will help others hold on. I hope my rehabilitation will show the doubters that life can be turned around. Of course, not every mental illness recedes, or is curable. Sometimes it leads people to do terrible things. But surely we, as a society, can learn never to abandon someone to the fog simply because it scares us.

One Sunday morning I was preparing to lead the Communion service in jail. The prisoners were filing in as usual, enjoying the chance to meet up with others from different wings – not *all* of them for nefarious purposes – and I was milling around with them. A word here, a handshake there, asking after a child, a court appearance, a letter.

"Hello, Miss" said the voice at my shoulder. "Miss" and "Guv" are the usual terms of address from prisoners to staff. I turned around and saw a dark-haired man, well-built, plump even. Smiling broadly. It was Viktor! "I'm back from hospital," he said, heavily accented. "I came to say thank you."

I shook his hand, warmly welcomed him, but inside I was gaping. This was incredible. Yes, he still had his sentence to serve, but… like the demon-possessed man Jesus is supposed to have healed, here was Viktor "clothed and in his right mind". He was never demon-possessed, of course, but the contrast to his former raving self was astonishing. Once again I was struck by the power of treatment and care.

INTO THE JUNGLE

Tough, urban music, often with hard, rap lyrics, seems to fit the average prisoner's experience and I often hear it blasting out as I walk around the wings. The emotion and anger that's so often expressed in this kind of music simmers just below the surface in jail, erupting every now and then with sometimes tragic consequences. Life after prison can be incredibly difficult too, often scary, hugely challenging – a bit like hacking through an almost impenetrable jungle. Apart from a very few offenders who have been sentenced to a whole life tariff, everyone currently serving a jail sentence will, eventually, be released. Far from being an end to the sentence, many are released on licence – in other words, subject to a period of compulsory supervision, meetings, even courses, with the risk of being sent back if they don't comply. No matter how reasonable and necessary this period is, it can still invoke a sense of pressure in the newly released prisoner. Then there are the ongoing personal effects of having been in jail. People freed after a long time inside must come to terms with changes in society, possibly the death and certainly the moving on of family members and friends, and the psychological impact of setting up a new life outside of an institution. In contrast to the lifers and long-termers, there are also large numbers of prisoners who serve short sentences. In recent times there has been plenty of public debate and comment about the so-called revolving door to jail, where short-sentenced prisoners seem stuck on a never-ending cycle of reoffending, their sentences not long enough to encourage reform and their community support and supervision too scant.

Clearly we can't lock up everyone and throw away the key. So if people are to resettle properly into a decent and law-abiding life, whatever the length of their recently completed sentence, somehow we must help that process along. It starts in jail, through interviews with probation officers, debt advisers, Job Centre workers. Chaplains are there from the start, trying to help someone make sense of the road so far; as well as charities and mentors, officers and teachers, authority and friend, carrot and stick. It's not always effective, there's not a lot of cash, and our subjects are not always willing. It's a stop and start process, and I think this is what gives a lot of people the impression that most attempts at rehabilitation fail. But I have come to see that measures of success are relative. Has someone stayed out of jail longer this time? Or been convicted of a lesser offence than before? That's progress! It can take years for someone to alter their habitual ways and although the process does indeed start in jail it has to carry on once that person is outside of the walls.

Walking out of the gates, whether it's for the first and only time or the umpteenth, is a bit like entering a jungle – but with all-too-human predators and dangers. Will the formerly addicted stay away from the pub and the pusher? Can the lifer cope with the fast pace? What will they do for money

– will they use legitimate means of income generation… or not? All of this set against the frequent public reaction of "There's no such thing as an 'ex' offender."

There is a recognized set of circumstances which need to be addressed if people are to negotiate the jungle effectively. These circumstances have been identified by research and are known as the "Seven pathways to resettlement". The pathways cover fundamental areas of life, and getting these right can be a way to stabilize an offender's place in society and thus reduce the likelihood of reoffending. They are accommodation; education, training, and employment; debt, benefits, and finance; health and personal care; drugs and alcohol; children and families; attitudes, thinking, and behaviour. A bit like Maslow's hierarchy of needs, an ex-offender is going to have a hard time establishing a stable and law-abiding life without a home, income, personal support, and a change in habits and lifestyle. If you think about it these things are the building blocks of *all* our lives. They give us a stake in society, a sense that we belong, and a reason for responsibility.

Housing and homelessness is a big issue – coming to jail may well mean the loss of a tenancy, or being kicked out of the family home – and for single men there's not a lot out there after release. A close family member of mine experienced a few days on the street as a young man – only a few days, but enough to see him hungry, threatened at knifepoint in a shelter, and sleeping on a bench in a churchyard in November. He had family to go back to, however sheepishly. For those who don't, or who lack the skills my relative had, the descent can be all too rapid. I remember talking with John, an ex-serviceman (so many ex-servicemen!), over endless cups of tea in the weeks prior to his release. He'd overcome the drink problem for now (having managed to stay away from anything illicit whilst inside and completing the detox programme). But he had no one and nowhere to go out to. And he was scared. It struck me as such a contrast – a guy who'd, presumably, been trained to be brave, now trembling at the prospect of going it alone. "In here," he said, almost apologetically, "I have a bed, food, company. Out there I have nothing." People have taken that both ways, of course. One reaction might be, "Lazy so and so, get a job, get off your arse, and start grafting for your needs." And it's true: I've met a fair few that I'd quite like to say that to. But not everyone.

These pathways, the fundamentals, are so often tightly wrapped around one another, like vines snaking up a tree. Where does one begin and the other end? Without a decent education, there is not much hope of a job. Without a supportive family, there is not much hope of education succeeding. Without a job, there will be no money, no home. Depression kicks in; drinking, drugs, which ruins families, creates more victims. Time and time again, I've found myself wishing I could turn back the clock and deal with the issues that confronted John, Danny, David, and all the others from their earliest days. Because it's in those childhood years that it all seems to begin, the trauma and deprivation, the bewilderment, the aggression. I have a colleague who used to be a senior teacher. She commented to me one day that she could tell from the first days of Reception class which children were already on a path of potential self-destruction.

On a happier note I've also found that, just as I did when faced with the custody case, the next generation of children can be the key driver for someone getting themselves sorted out. A supportive family can be hugely influential and there are many young women who are doing a sterling job of bringing up the kids while dad's inside, at the same time trying to influence their partner to get their act together. I remember one girlfriend telling me that she simply loved her boyfriend, and despite the difficulties and her intense frustration with him she was sticking by him in the hope that he would eventually grow up. I hope he does, and I hope he comes to realize he's a lucky man. Some of them do manage it, once they've been confronted with reality. Yes, there are those men I meet who seem to have babies all over the place with their several girlfriends, but there are also those who are brought up short by missing their baby's birth, or an important birthday, or yet another Christmas. Often these men want to be good parents but have no idea how.

"Storybook Dads" is a genius idea belonging to Sharon Berry. In 2002 she was working as a volunteer in HMP Channings Wood and saw how maintaining family ties had such a positive impact on prisoners. She developed the idea of prisoners recording stories for their children, and after her relocation to HMP Dartmoor she set up the charity Storybook Dads in 2003. Statistics on the Storybook Dads (and now Mums) website state that 50% of serving prisoners lose contact with their children but those who do maintain contact are six times less likely to reoffend.

I came across Storybook Dads at a conference on reducing reoffending in London in 2010. The idea of Storybook Dads/Mums is that a prisoner is recorded reading a story to his or her child, that recording is then edited, sound effects and music are added, and the resulting creation is burnt onto a CD and sent to the child. The parent is thus helped to play a part in the child's life, and may even find his or her own literacy skills improved. The child has a vital link with an absent parent, positively affecting self-esteem and feelings of security, which in turn may help to divert another generation from the cycle of offending.

I thought this was brilliant. By then I was already freelancing from home in my spare time as a voiceover artist, and had learnt the basics of voice recording and editing. I could see that with my existing skills, and my role in the prison where I was working, Storybook Dads could enhance the efforts we were already making towards supporting rehabilitation. I had to put together a business case, fully costed (it was only a few hundred pounds for the basic recording equipment), and work out the logistics of having a recording device and SIM card in a High Security jail (!). But before long we were in business.

Jim came across as an old-school prisoner. Approaching middle age, stocky, he had crew-cut hair, tattoos, and an estuary accent. He'd applied to take part in the Storybook scheme and turned up for his appointment with me in a room close to the chapel which had been set up for the project. As I called him down the corridor I could see he was nervous so as we sat down I tried to put him at ease. We chatted about his kids, about the fact that he hardly saw them now, but his ex had given permission for him to send this recording, which was a positive sign. In the room was a table full of children's books – short stories like *The Very Hungry Caterpillar*. These lent themselves to the addition of sound effects and had been carefully chosen by me. Permission to use them in these recordings had also very generously been given by the publishers.

Jim looked at the books, then at me. "There's a problem," he said, hesitantly. "I can't read."

Ah.

But thanks to the wonders of technology, Jim's problem was no problem. I set the recorder going, then simply read the words, line by line, and Jim repeated them after me. Later, I told him, as I edited, my voice would disappear, and all that would be left would be Jim, telling the story. I could see that he wasn't convinced, but I knew that when I invited him back a week later to hear the finished product he'd be delighted.

Delighted wasn't the word. As his voice unfolded from the speakers Jim's eyes grew wide and then finally he burst into tears. "I've never done anything like that before," he gulped, "Never read a story to my kids, because I couldn't. Thank you so much."

In the weeks that followed, not only did Jim's kids write to him, but he also started a prison literacy course, and eventually he came back to that little room and recorded another story – only this time he didn't need me to say a word.

Like so many other men I've worked with I have no idea what happened to Jim. But I like to think that small victory led onto other, greater ones. Jim would have his own jungle to negotiate, but maybe I'd helped him hack down a few vines in his way.

It's a hugely daunting process, rebuilding a life that for all intents and purposes has crumbled to bits. I had my kids, a remnant of friends and family, but it became very apparent after my gradual emerging from illness that I could not stay in the parish where I had suffered the breakdown. This was underlined on the very first Sunday I returned to the church. I hadn't preached, or even played a big part, but as I was mingling afterwards, a parishioner (who herself had had significant issues over the years) began screeching invective at me: how dare I call myself a Christian; I wasn't fit to be a minister; I had a cheek turning up in church after all I'd done.

"I'm sorry you feel that way," I muttered, and left with as much dignity as I could muster (not very much). My letter of resignation was despatched to the vicar that evening – and, I have to say, readily accepted. The trouble is, of course, when you're a clergy type, the house goes with the job. So now, after all the personal disruption, and only two years into ordained life, I had to throw myself on the mercy of the bishop, for a new job and a home to go with it.

A job and a home did come and, although the ladder I was climbing was a bit wobbly, life settled for a while. I was still taking medication, although my stubborn determination to wean myself off it eventually succeeded. I have to say I felt so much better once I stopped taking the drugs. I would never suggest to anyone to stop their meds but I have wondered in the time since whether in fact the anti-depressants and anti-psychotics (which seemed to be changed every few months) had actually contributed to my fragmented state. The children were wonderful, loving and resilient, but I knew there remained quite a job to do in rebuilding their sense of security. And in many ways I was no less vulnerable myself. But the new church was vibrant, welcoming, creative, and the curate's house that came with it was lovely. My work flourished, I made friends, and I began to look forward to life as a vicar of my own parish one day.

Quite often when I'm visiting the new arrivals into the prison (something we must do every day) I'll meet someone who's been in once, twice or even more before. It's hard to know how to react. Do I grin along with them, greet them with a wink and say, "So, you're back then," or do I shake my head and ask what on earth went wrong? Often it depends on what I know of their nature and offending; on many occasions I come up with a mixture of both. Whilst there are offenders who serve their time and leave, duly chastened, never to be seen again, for the vast majority of low-level offenders, there's a long road ahead of making mistakes, not addressing issues, and walking blithely into self-made traps. It might take several years of repeat offending, although possibly on a lesser scale, followed by a lengthy period reflecting on their own stupidity before they are truly able to make a fresh start.

I mention this now because once again my life seems to have followed a course designed to teach me a lesson. Here I was, new house, new job, health slowly returning, kids settling. And I rush into a relationship with the first man who takes an interest.

What on earth was I thinking? Hindsight and all that. I've rationalized it since (I had plenty of time). I was still very vulnerable, and I'd received no counselling at all as part of my recovery. Issues still lay unaddressed, demons unchallenged. I was still hurting profoundly after the breakdown of my marriage, and when my ex remarried quickly the hurt was compounded. I'd felt rejected by the previous parish as well as by several friends and relations. Years later I can see that I wanted to demonstrate to the world that someone wanted me – and at the same time didn't really believe that anyone would.

My beau was another vicar, himself emerging from a painful marriage breakdown and, with hindsight, facing as many unresolved issues as me. We gravitated towards one another in friendship, which developed along inevitable lines, and much to the disapproval of several onlookers. I don't blame them now but at the time adversity only drove us together more. I had my doubts over the two years we courted, and so did he. But we ploughed on, convinced ourselves all was well, and certainly had some very good times together. We were married in a joyful ceremony in 2002, and I moved from the city church where I'd been an assistant priest to join him some distance away in the rural parish he had recently taken up. With a successful couple of years of ministry under my belt, and after a conversation I'd had with senior clergy before the move, I expected to take up my own parish role somewhere nearby within a very short time.

But, in a horrible re-running of history, that parish never emerged. In fact it soon became clear that it was never going to emerge. At that time, unbeknown to us, the bishop of the diocese we moved to generally didn't approve of married couples both having paid clergy jobs, and he seemed more specifically not to approve of me. My appeal to him resulted in a letter explaining that he wanted to ensure the stability of this second marriage. I think in his well-meaning attempt to do so, by placing us into traditional roles, he inadvertently made the whole situation ten times worse.

So here I was once again, watching my husband go about his vicarly duties, while I was not able to fulfil my own deeply felt, hard won, vocation. Instead I seemed to be pushed back into the role of "Vicar's wife" – a role I had resisted right at the beginning.

But I was *not* going to get depressed again. And I didn't. Perhaps I was being selfish, but I was angry. Angry and weary of what I saw as years of institutional sexism. Angry at myself for being so naïve. Angry at my own impotence. Angry at God for dumping me (as I saw it). I made contact with other women clergy up and down the country, several of whom reported similar experiences. I wrote letters. I made a fuss. My efforts had about as much effect as tickling a mountain.

I had given my life to this institution but I felt frozen out. Over the next couple of years I persisted sporadically but unsuccessfully – job applications seemed to get nowhere, and at one time, expecting a baby, I was advised by a clergyman that I shouldn't apply for a particular job because I was pregnant. This was aside from the rules that required a vicar to live in the parish – as I was living with my husband in *his* parish I was automatically disqualified. We used to joke bitterly that we'd be better off if we divorced.

I say we joked. Actually we realized fairly early on that we had made a colossal mistake. We struggled to find an area of compatibility, and once the honeymoon mist cleared from our eyes, we found our values and takes on life to be poles apart. But to split was unthinkable. Quite apart from the sincerity of the promises we made, and our wish to fulfil them, it would be a disaster. For each of us personally, and as time went on, for two little ones born to us, as well as for my older children still living at home. And yes, for our careers too – well, such as existed of mine. I knew if I divorced again at that stage I could kiss goodbye to any hope of ever working as a parish priest. And in any case, we lived in his vicarage – I would be truly jobless and homeless this time – hardly an option with four kids. Trapped by circumstance, we resolved to live together as best we could, in friendship if possible.

I still needed to work: I didn't have the luxury of opting out and, in any case, that's never been my style. So I was working long hours anyway, just not in the job I was qualified for. I couldn't see how that was any more supportive of a marriage. I worked for two church related charities in those years – one large and international, then, having been made redundant, one small and local. I was not a great success at either. I supplemented my income with freelance voiceover work, done in the wee small hours when the kids were in bed, together with the broadcasting work that was beginning to emerge. But it was far from what I wanted to be doing and I continued to long for what I saw as a proper job as a priest – the role for which I'd been trained and had given so many years of my life. I felt completely lost and very alone.

Again, remembering all these years of struggle, and the mental strength I had to find, makes me realize how hard it is for ex-offenders as they are thrust into the jungle of the real world. It's hard to believe you're capable of so much but not to be given a chance; to feel isolated; to be confused about where you belong and where you're going, still fighting a stigma from past events. It would be so easy to give up, to hate those who seem to be blocking you, to retreat into despair or bitterness. At an event where rehabilitation was discussed between criminal justice practitioners and former prisoners, one man asked, "When will I stop being an ex-offender?" In other words, when will I cease to be defined by the worst bits of my life, and instead regain an identity as an individual with worth and potential?

How ironic that it should be prison which gave that identity to me. I saw an ad in the local paper, for a chaplain to a brand new institution. This was to be a Secure Training Centre – a privately run establishment for young people aged 12 to 17, who had been given detention orders by the youth courts. I had a background in law, I'd been the minister for young people in the city church, I had the necessary qualifications – and I secured the job.

A number of times in the years since that interview I've come across the notion that, if you're a successful clergyperson, you secure a plum parish not long after college, gradually moving up the ranks and in the right circles until you reach a senior position. If you're less successful but still OK, you spend your working years in a series of perfectly respectable parishes, doing a good job before a quiet retirement. If you blot your copybook somewhere along the way (divorce, dodgy theology, upset someone powerful) you become a hospital (or maybe school) chaplain. And if you're really at the bottom of the vicar food chain you end up in jail – as a prison chaplain.

I vehemently oppose that view (of course), although it certainly exists in places. An acquaintance was told she couldn't possibly have the right qualities for a church job because she had only ever been a prison chaplain. A number of chaplain colleagues struggle to get their local church structures to take any notice of their work – although I have to say my current batch of bishops are very supportive and HMP Bedford even had a visit from the Archbishop of Canterbury in 2015.

Any clergy job is tougher than people presume but jail demands a particular skill. Every day my prison chaplain colleagues and I stand on a kind of front line. We're meeting people from some of the most deprived, even depraved, backgrounds; on a daily basis we deal with the direct consequences of violence, poverty, hopelessness, and fear. Prison is a place where even a hint of ******** is rumbled in minutes. I need to keep my wits about me, whilst retaining compassion. I must be quick-thinking, theologically agile, open-minded, non-judgmental. Within the sometimes stifling boundaries of the hierarchy, I need to find a way to be independent, to remain true to my beliefs whilst they are challenged from every angle. Going about my daily duties I've been laughed at, spat at, cursed, and cat-called. I've also had the most amazing encounters, sitting with people at deeply affecting moments in their lives. I've been cried on, called for, questioned, and trusted.

I've already said this isn't a book primarily about faith, nor about theology. But my own faith is at the heart of what I do and why I do it. I truly believe that for a religion to have any meaning, it must face the darkest corners of society, the hardest parts of life. My interpretation of the Christian faith is that it is not about judging people, nor even about persuading others to believe what you do. It's about helping others walk along their own personal pathway, as you yourself stumble with them. It's about bringing light to darkness, hope to despair. And yes, it's about accountability too: responsibility, acknowledging wrongdoing, changing your tune. From those first days in that youth establishment, when I met kids with dull eyes, already convinced that life was "them and us", I've tried to put forward an alternative.

There was a young girl I spent a lot of time with in that first job – Nicky. She was only 14 when she came into custody, for a particularly nasty attack on another girl. Nicky had been in care for a number of years, her mother fighting her own battles and unable to care for her adequately. Nicky was a hard nut – or so she thought. She bad-mouthed the custody staff, was disruptive in the compulsory lessons, tried to make me flinch with her language. But it was obvious that she had never had someone stick by her and so, scared and hurt, she made sure she never depended on anyone again. A reasonable strategy, in many ways, and one I've used myself for much of my life. But I wanted her to learn that you could be independent, and yet also connect. Bad connections, bad relationships, are the most destructive thing imaginable, but good connections, the gradual development of trust, can change the entire horizon.

I didn't talk religion with Nicky. I played board games. We listened to music. We made things together – little craft projects. The kind of things I had done with my own daughter, of a similar age. And importantly, I turned up – when I said I would. When she was upset, or badly-behaved, when she swore at me, or threw a tantrum, I still turned up the next day; and the next and the next. Eventually she asked me why I did it, why I bothered with someone like her. And I was able to tell her about my motivations – to attempt to give her care, understanding, and love. I did it because of my faith, but I didn't do it to get her to follow my faith. That was her choice. As the weeks went by she asked more and more about that faith of mine, and so, yes, I did then start to talk about it, about its central characters, about its (not always commendable) history, and about its fundamental message of hope. I simply walked alongside that young woman, not giving up on her, while she explored what she wanted.

In time, Nicky was baptized in the chapel of the secure training centre, with her mother and her social worker in attendance. When she left, she was allowed to return to her home, to live with her mother. And both Nicky and her mother had already met their local vicar on a number of occasions, who was ready and willing to take up the walk with them.

I've been criticized for concentrating on prisoners, accused of forgetting the victims. Never! I've been one too. The impact of violence or theft, rape or murder is horrendous and long-lasting, throwing out ripples of disruption which can last generations. There are prisoners I meet whose offences disgust me, whose attitudes appal me. But we gain nothing by demonizing every offender, or by distancing ourselves from sometimes all-too-human behaviour. Where we can understand, divert, heal, and forgive, I believe we create more ripples, which themselves can change the lives of generations.

Since 2013 I've been a patron of No Offence – a network of individuals and organizations dedicated to promoting constructive approaches to crime and rehabilitation. The organization has established an annual event – the Redemption and Justice Awards. These awards celebrate often unsung heroes or unacknowledged work which is done to help ex-offenders battle their way through the post-release jungle, often by people who have been in the system themselves. I've been so impressed with the range of initiatives I've seen, from projects to keep kids off the streets to bringing dogs into prison cells. Time and again I've heard the recipients of these awards talk about the importance of someone giving them a chance, trusting they could change and that they could help others to change too. That chance is sometimes a job, or a start-up grant, at other times it's mentoring, training or support. It's always belief in them as a person of potential.

I baptized Steve one Easter morning at the main chapel service. He'd had problems with alcohol for much of his adult life, having started drinking on street corners in his early teens. He didn't know his dad, his mum struggled with mental health problems, he wasn't great at school. He'd drink and get into fights, he'd have complicated relationships which also led to fights with other men, and finally he was put away for GBH, having seriously injured another man outside a pub. This meant leaving behind his girlfriend and his little son – another single mum left to struggle with a disaffected kid and all the potential for trouble that held. In prison Steve could be aggressive, quick to react, and often in trouble. Just another con going nowhere.

He came to a chapel event one day, because he'd heard there would be food (a pretty common reason for attendance!). Much to his surprise he liked the service:

there were songs, poems, ideas couched in terms he could relate to. And yes, food! Steve's curiosity was piqued, and he returned. Over several months he came, and attended our small discussion group too. He undertook a distance-learning Bible study course. He asked questions; he was challenging; he struggled to look at life in a different way. In all of this Steve was welcomed and taken seriously, accepted, despite the damage his behaviour had caused.

Steve's girlfriend visited regularly – so often I wonder if these girls know what they're getting themselves into, but the impact of a stable, sensible woman can have a hugely beneficial effect. She, too, had started attending the local church, mainly the Mums and Toddlers group, and was finding the welcome there helpful. She wanted to get their son christened, and was wondering about it for herself.

Usually I prefer to run a short course of preparation before I baptize (or christen) anyone, child or adult. But that Easter weekend I'd been woken by a strange dream and the firm notion that I should simply offer to baptize people during the Sunday morning service, even without preparation.

Most of our Sunday services are attended by about 50 or so men. That's a pretty good percentage of a 500 strong population. Sure, it's a captive audience, and I know that some come for a bit of, shall we say, "Sunday trading". But by and large the guys are there because they want to be – they're curious, or in need, or genuinely practising their faith. Nevertheless, it's a daunting sea of faces when you stand up at the front, even for an old hand like me. How much more for a nervous young prisoner, about to declare in front of his peers that he's a believer. But that's just what Steve did, alongside four others, that Easter Sunday morning, when I offered the opportunity. The men had been a bit shocked at first, and so had my volunteers. They were used to me and my crazy ideas, but this was distinctly off grid. I explained what baptism was, what it meant, how serious it was. There was silence for a while. "Have I completely misjudged this?" I thought. Finally, Steve stood up, then another and another.

It's one thing to christen a baby in front of adoring family and friends – I love it (and quite miss it these days); the frilly robe, the delighted parents, the mischievous older sibling. But it's quite another experience to baptize convicted criminals, big, solid lads, in front of a roomful of blokes and a handful of (usually) cynical prison officers. One of the funny bits is the fact that most of them seem to wear rock-solid hair gel – I get spiked when I'm splashing the water on their heads.

But it was overwhelming to see these men come up, make themselves vulnerable. They don't have to do it, there's certainly no pressure. It's incredibly moving, to see them yearning for a new start and a better life. Being baptized was an important statement for them to make – "I'm trying to change." But it's an important statement for me, as a representative of the church, too – "Despite all that has happened, all that you have done or not done, I, we, believe in you."

Steve left us a few weeks after his baptism. He bumped into one of my colleagues in town a while later – his son and girlfriend got baptized too, a wedding was in the offing, he was working, attending church. A family had been created, a child was less likely to follow in his father's footsteps, a man restored. Those fundamentals were in place – home, job, income, family, health, attitude. It's not always, or even often, like that, but when it does happen, when those positive ripples spread out, you know that it is just possible to beat the tigers in the jungle.

CHAPTER 8

PARALLEL LINES

Red and yellow and pink and green, orange and...

"Purple!" I piped up, proud of my one word in my first stage appearance – at four years old. It's still my favourite colour (not the bishop-y kind; despite many kind comments, that's *never* going to be me. Anyway, I think bishops' shirts are pink, not proper purple). I suppose in one way or another I've been a performer ever since. Mind you, I wasn't that impressed being cast as the donkey in one year's nativity play. And the next year wasn't much better in my opinion – I suppose the narrator *was* a plum job – on stage the whole time. But no costume! Everyone else had sparkles and glitter and wings and tea-towels and crowns. I had to wear a boring day dress.

I've always loved dressing up, drawn to colour and drama. When I was eight I attended a Roman Catholic convent school in Guildford. The nuns were lovely, especially Sister P., the Mother Superior. For some reason she took me under her wing and we would sometimes spend break-times strolling across the beautiful playing field, just chatting. I was very fond of her. Every Monday morning, Catholic or not, we all trooped to the church next door for Mass. The priest had gorgeous robes, the incense, the hymns – I wasn't a Catholic, in fact my family didn't attend church at all, but I enjoyed the spectacle and understood that there was something special about the occasion. One Monday morning I decided I didn't like being left out when all the Catholic girls went up for Communion. If this God fella was handing out blessings, I wanted a few!

Up to the rail I tripped, knelt down, face upturned, mouth open expectantly. The priest moved along the line of little girls, dispensing wafers onto tongues. He stepped in front of me, and hesitated. He didn't recognize me. Sister P. was by his side, put a hand on his arm and gently shook her head. They passed on by. Confused and upset, I returned to my pew. Some of my classmates nudged each other and giggled. "You shouldn't have gone up," whispered Kathy. "Why not?" I retorted. "I wanted a piece of God."

All these years later, I welcome all kinds to the communion table. I don't ask if they're baptized, I don't care what age they are, who they are. If they come, and want a piece of God, then hallelujah. That's not to be disrespectful to my Catholic colleagues – they have their rules and I'm not drumming up conflict with them. Sometimes it's almost funny to see some of the prisoners shuffle up to the communion table. They don't really know what they're doing, I can see them looking sideways at the ones who do, and when it comes to their turn for the bread, they look like frightened rabbits as they take the wafer or the morsel of loaf. But they've come. Something has pulled them out of their seat and up to the front, to this odd woman in strange robes who's been spouting on about heaven and new beginnings. I never forget the confusion of an eight-year-old being sent back empty-handed.

There's another picture that comes to mind from that year I was eight. I did love dressing up, and had a tumbled boxful of scarves, plastic necklaces and old floppy hats. On one occasion I found a big cardboard box, took it to my room and turned it upside down. I covered the "table" it made in a tea-towel. Then I rummaged around, and at the bottom of my dressing-up box found an old dress of my mother's. (Ha! It was pinky-purple.) I slipped it on over my clothes. Then taking my tea-set, I laid out a plate and a cup on the makeshift "altar" and coerced my brother to come into my room and stand there while I "celebrated communion". This was 1974, long before women priests were allowed. Nevertheless, it was the first ever appearance of "Glamvicar"!

The outward expressions of religion faded not long after that (although I never stopped believing in God), but the love of clothes didn't. I felt so restricted as I grew up that I used colour and grooming as an act of defiance. I think it's no coincidence, and sadly symbolic, that my mother frequently insisted I wear old, dark, unfashionable clothing as I entered my teenage years. But I usually managed to persuade her to let me wear something dressy for school mufti days – my classmates would ask me if I even owned a pair of jeans.

And my various schools did provide me with wonderful opportunities to explore the performer in me. There were plays and concerts, choirs and even elocution lessons. Every time an elderly lady thanks me for my sermon, of which she could hear every word, I think back to Mrs C., the elocution teacher, and thank her silently. Those lessons led on to poetry recitals and to public-speaking competitions.

This reached its height in my final year at school. Every year we entered a team into the English Speaking Union's Public Speaking Competition. Teams consisted of a chairperson, a main speaker, and a deliverer of the vote of thanks. I'd been the main speaker in my penultimate year, making it to the London finals, but getting no further. This year we entered again, with me as the main speaker, my best friend as the chair, and another classmate to give the vote of thanks. We made it to the London finals again. They were held at the HQ of the English Speaking Union, at Dartmouth House, in Mayfair. Amidst the grand surroundings, with glistening chandeliers and eminent judges, we took to the podium. My friend introduced me eloquently, and then it was my turn. I adjusted my newly purchased grey, silky suit, picked up my cue cards, smiled around the room, and began.

"Nuts! Whole hazelnuts!"

Heads jerked slightly; eyes widened; one judge smiled to himself. I'd seized their attention. The next few minutes were an exploration of the tactics of the advertisers, starting from that well-known opening line of an ad for a chocolate bar. Questions duly parried afterwards, the vote of thanks having been offered, we three young ladies left the podium, to listen to other competitors and await the verdict at the end of the evening.

We won. A trophy, a certificate, and a place in the national finals: for a short while I was no longer the awkward, non-sporty, off-centre lonely girl. I had actually won something, I had a talent. I could distil ideas, use inspiring words and images. I could communicate.

There have been times when I wished I had better careers guidance at that stage. Thwarted from taking a creative degree, my entry into the legal world was a way of using my communication skills but it didn't ignite my passion. When I look back now and put events into context, with a bit of steering and a bit of confidence I might have made it into radio at that point. Like many London teenagers of the late 70s and early 80s, I was transfixed by Capital Radio. I'd listen to it every available hour, on a little red transistor radio, often hidden under my pillow. "Little" Nicky Horne, Graham Dene, Richard Allinson, Kenny Everett – in the spirit of all great radio, it felt as if they were my friends, and they were certainly my inspirational teachers. I made up my own radio shows, recording them on one of those flat-bed tape recorders: pressing play and record simultaneously and hoping the birds tweeting in the tree outside my window didn't come across too loudly on the finished product. I'd make mix tapes with selections from the Top 40, and create my own news features and jingles. The music scene was dramatic and varied at the time – moving from glam rock into punk, then ska, and the New Romantics. Radio was in its heyday, and I lived in one of the most vibrant cities in the world.

But it was not to be. I had to wait another 20 years for my accidental break into radio.

I was working in a city-centre church in 2001, the happy days after recovering from my breakdown. The church had a very good choir led by a talented but eccentric choirmaster. He'd rehearse his singers for hours – they really did look like they were fit to drop sometimes. But by golly they were good. I'm not sure how, but a producer for the BBC World Service got to hear of this choir and came to the church to record a service featuring their music. They brought a lead presenter with them, John Newbury, who was also an experienced radio broadcaster. But they also wanted a minister from the church to help lead a bit of the service, and I think more by luck than judgment I was the person available. I wrote some prayers and, when called upon, did my bit in front of the microphone. All those adolescent years of public-speaking plus the legal and clergy training stood me in good stead, and I seemed to go down well. Chatting with John afterwards, he commented that I came across as very relaxed in front of the mic. I joked about my (still unfulfilled) ambition to read the news. He told me he had connections with BBC Radio's Religion and Ethics team, and promised to recommend me to the head of the team, Christine Morgan.

I was grateful but thought nothing of it. The broadcast went out on the World Service and that was that.

John did send an email to Christine and she made initial contact saying she would consider me. But I heard no more and in any case became rather side-tracked by getting married and having a baby. It wasn't until early 2004, frustrated by the position I found myself in with the church and lack of parish, that I contacted her again. The next thing I knew I received an email from a producer asking me to write a pilot script for the overnight version of *Pause for Thought* on Radio 2. Yikes!

I still have the email as well as the initial briefing notes and my first attempts at a script. The slot was no more than 2 minutes long, and went out on weeknights at 1:30 a.m., during Janice Long's show, repeated at 3:30 a.m. with Alex Lester. Thankfully they were pre-recorded – although that made it more difficult to sound seamless, as you had no idea what would have gone before. The briefing notes gave me a context, stating: "The programmes in which night time *Pause for Thought* (PFT) sits are fast moving, and make no concessions to insomniacs… about a quarter of a million people will hear the weekday PFTs… the age range is 19 upwards, but they are more likely to be in their 30s–40s. Predominantly male, they will be going about their business – travelling, returning late from evenings out, shift workers, students, truckers."

A few years after this I was amused to be on an overnight ferry to France when, although it wasn't me on the radio that time, I heard the slot played out over the public speakers. I smiled to myself at the oddness of realizing some nights it was *my* voice reaching the ears of passengers and crew. Odder still, the night my youngest child was born, in 2006, I had been unable to sleep. The baby was two weeks late, and I was due in the hospital for an induction the following morning. Sitting at home in bed, I had just finished listening to myself deliver the PFT, when the first labour pains started. Two hours later, just as the repeat was playing, I had a delivery of another kind – a baby girl in my arms.

One of the things I always appreciated about the DJs in my teenage days had been the way they seemed like my friends as I was listening. It wasn't just the words they said, but the friendly, personal tone too. Early on in my broadcasting career I learned the knack to this. A lawyer or a priest is usually addressing large numbers of people and has a message to deliver to the group as a whole. This leads to a certain type of declaratory delivery, speech-making in effect. A radio broadcaster is usually addressing large numbers too – millions even – but the trick is to speak as if you're addressing each listener individually. I was advised to imagine one person I could be speaking to – even bring a picture of them into the studio while I was learning. I didn't need the photo but I did imagine my dad. I think he has listened to just about every broadcast I have ever done (and that's quite a lot now) and it was his imagined face that taught me how to achieve that conversational approach.

The producer I worked with in those early days, Janet McLarty, was lovely, becoming a personal friend – and godmother to that baby girl eventually. She believed in my broadcasting ability and gave me every opportunity to learn and develop. She badgered the senior people on my behalf and in 2006 she produced a *Sunday Worship* programme for Radio 4, on Remembrance Sunday, with me leading.

It was my first taste of live radio and I was in my element. I loved the rehearsals beforehand, the split-second timing, the coming together of all the different parts, the script-writing, the delivery. My baby daughter was only a few weeks old at this stage, and I was feeding her myself, so the need to make sure I factored *that* into the schedule added another layer of, shall we say, excitement. I was nervous because I knew a lot of people would be listening and, as it was live, what was said stayed said; but once I got going it was no different to the many speeches I had given, or indeed, church services I had led. Somehow I was able to filter out the mics and the wires and, although I had to keep a close eye on the clock, it all went smoothly. Immediately after the service Janet received a text message from the senior producer to say well done to us all. He was notoriously difficult to please so it felt like a triumph indeed.

I'd worked with the senior producer before – on Janet's recommendation, he had rather warily tried me out for the *Prayer for the Day* slot early in the morning on Radio 4. I remember the first time I recorded this with him, I was in a studio local to where I was living, and he was in a studio in Manchester. The studios were connected up through an ISDN line – a particularly high-quality phone line capable of transmitting sound at recordable quality. The studio I was in wasn't the best – the soundproofing was pretty rubbish, and the mic wasn't great. The producer wasn't very happy with it and kept stopping and starting the recording, making me deliver lines over and over again until he was satisfied with the sound. I was eight months pregnant with that baby girl and I began to get very tired. The final straw came when the producer stopped me mid-sentence and said, "We need to do this one all over again – you're breathing too loudly." I couldn't help myself. "I'm eight months pregnant!" I protested. "I'm doing my very best but with a baby taking up most of my lung space, there's not a lot I can do." After we'd finished and he'd gone off line, I ripped off my headphones and sat in the studio and sobbed.

He's a perfectionist, but he kept me on, and even included some of my offerings in a Radio 4 compilation book, so I can't have been all bad. We have a friendly professional relationship now, and he's given me some great opportunities, including another *Sunday Worship* in 2009, which went on to win an award the following year.

This was the broadcast I referred to earlier, for World Mental Health Day, about my personal experience of a breakdown and its aftermath. It was broadcast live on 11th October 2009, from Emmanuel Church, Didsbury. Along with a fellow broadcaster, Andrew Graystone and another great producer, Simon Vivian (who himself has now trained as a vicar), we explored the spiritual side of mental ill-health and challenged the reaction and stigma too often seen. The following year the programme was shortlisted for the Sandford St Martin Awards – a prestigious nomination for awards covering all broadcast media in religious and ethical matters. The ceremony was to be held at Lambeth Palace. Attending was a logistical nightmare for me – not only was I in the middle of a week's holiday in rural Devon, but I was on crutches as I'd torn my Achilles tendon whilst at a boot camp-style fitness session. I did go, we didn't win, but it was great to get the certificate of commendation. So I was surprised when we were then nominated for a Jerusalem Award – these are for specifically Christian programming. I trotted back up to London, almost a year after the original broadcast, looking forward to an enjoyable evening of networking, a buffet, and not much more. I was stunned when our programme was announced as a winner. I've had some pretty fantastic events happen in my life but that was one of my proudest moments.

Little by little I built up my capital with BBC Radio. I made a point of always saying "Yes" when they asked if I could do something and then working out afterwards how on earth I would manage to deliver! As the opportunities came, I was also looking after two teenagers and two little ones, running my own voiceover business, and starting out in prisons. Juggling indeed.

The voiceover work has been a fascinating side-line. Over the space of several months I had seen the same newspaper ad for training in voiceovers. Although it drew my eye, I dismissed it as probably a scam. But when my despair over what to do next was at its height I decided to take the plunge. I'd always been told I had a good speaking voice, so why not? I contacted the name on the ad, Gary Terzza, who turned out to be an experienced voiceover artist, a continuity announcer for Channel 4, and an altogether lovely chap. We met at a studio in rural Hertfordshire and he took me through my paces for three hours. It was hard work. But it was huge fun too, and at the end of the morning I had a demo CD filled with my voice, selling body lotion, sharing the traffic news, and exploring the wonders of the universe in a pretend documentary. He showed me how to create a profile on a voiceover website, and how to upload the demo. From there I could audition for voiceover jobs as they were advertised.

Over the next couple of years I provided the voice for an online training course for NATO troops going to Afghanistan, for the telephone hold message for several swanky hotels in Dubai ("Your call *is* important to us…"), a safety video for oil rigs, several radio ads, a web-ad for breast enlargement (!), and training modules for the European Union. Often I'd record late at night, once the kids were in bed and there was little noise outside. This was important because nearly all the recording was done at home, using a hand held digital recorder. I would then edit the sound using a free downloaded programme on my computer. At one stage, when I had a particularly long and demanding set of recordings to do, I set up a recording booth in a cupboard. Lined with duvets to deaden the sound, I could stand upright in it. I rigged up the mic, and a clip-on spotlight so I wasn't recording in the dark. It worked pretty well, but I did have to keep coming out for air every few minutes or so – the combination of spotlight, body heat, and duvets made it more of a sauna than a recording booth. I taught myself huge amounts about sound recording during those years, which has stood me in good stead. I've since used those skills to record and edit interviews for radio, to run a branch of Storybook Dads (as we have seen), and even to create Christmas presents for my kids.

By the time of the Jerusalem award I had also established myself as a presenter for the *Daily Service*, which goes out on Radio 4 longwave at 9:45 a.m. every weekday. This is the longest running religious programme in the world, having started in 1928 after the success of a campaign by Miss Kathleen Cordeux to have a short daily act of worship broadcast on the radio. Funnily enough, during the war the *Daily Service* was based in Bedford. These days I travel to

Manchester, as the programme usually goes out live from Emmanuel Church, in Didsbury.

I did not distinguish myself the first time I presented this programme in 2007. I was so nervous, and the environment felt so alien, that my voice tightened up and I sounded like a gruesome parody of Her Majesty. Indeed one listener wrote in to say how dreadful I was. I'm truly grateful to that senior producer for letting me have another go and for the guidance I received.

It *is* a skill that has to be learned – and this particular slot was nowhere near as informal as the overnight *Pause for Thought*. So I had to learn to combine the reverence of an act of worship with personal warmth for the individual listener, as well as say something of depth to people for whom the programme was a spiritual lifeline. Over the years I've had lovely letters from listeners from all over the world, many of whom are isolated, whether by age, language, or culture. The *Daily Service* is a vital link for them and a support in their lives. I've even heard of people living in countries where Christianity is illegal, who listen to the broadcast in secret, at great risk to themselves. When I stop to think about it, that's an awesome responsibility we presenters have, and a serious commendation for the public service remit of the BBC.

I must have mastered it because, nearly a decade on, I'm still asked to present the programme from time to time. It's quite a challenge, this one, because it's only 15 minutes long and goes to the top of the hour. Woe betide any presenter who crashes the pips!

We deal with this by having a meticulous rehearsal. After a while you get used to roughly how long the script needs to be but we time the rehearsal to the second. The broadcast has to finish at 9:59 and 50 secs on the dot, so we will cut (or, more rarely, insert) words, lines, whole paragraphs, or hymn verses, to get the timing exact. But we still have to be on our toes when it comes to the live transmission, because any number of events could throw our timings out. The continuity announcer could take a few seconds longer announcing the programme, so we start a little late. The music could inadvertently speed up or slow down. The presenter could speak a little faster or slower than in the rehearsal. For this reason the presenter, sitting in the body of the church, wears cans (headphones) connected to the producer in the back room, with the sound equipment. The producer and the broadcast assistant watch the seconds closely, and advise the presenter, through the cans, of any adjustments needed. There have been times when I've been saying one sentence, and listening to the producer saying something else, whilst calculating timings and composing an amended sentence, all at the same time! It is like the proverbial swan gliding along, whilst paddling furiously underneath. I've had occasions when the timings have been miscalculated, or the continuity announcer has come across early. There's been a sound blackout, where the signal was lost, but we had to carry on broadcasting until it came back. And times when a significant event has happened overnight, and the entire script has to be rewritten in the early hours of the morning. Even after all these years, the relief when we get to the pips successfully is wonderful. I was hugely proud to have been described by one of the *Daily Service* producers as bombproof – although I'm glad not to have that tested too often.

Quite often, when I was the designated driver on the school run rota, and before I got involved in radio myself, I'd listen to Terry Wogan on Radio 2 on my way back home. I usually tuned in just before the *Pause for Thought* slot. I liked the *Breakfast Show*, because it was varied and often funny. I wasn't so sure about the PFT slot – sometimes it worked, sometimes it didn't. There were times when I'd groan at a familiar name and turn off; other times I'd hear someone I could relate to so I'd stay tuned. Even after I began to present the night-time slot, I never imagined myself on the *Breakfast Show*. This was hallowed ground and, I thought, out of my league. My dad used to tease me and say, "When you're on with Terry…" "Yeah, yeah, Dad," I'd reply, "like, never."

I suppose I was right in a way, because I never did appear with Terry Wogan. But a few months after Chris Evans took over the *Breakfast Show*, the Religion and Ethics department once again got in touch and offered me a pilot *Pause for Thought* on the programme. If my reaction to getting the night time PFT was "Yikes", this time it was "OMG!"

The first time I did it, I was truly nervous: shakingly, stomach-churningly nervous. I was up at the crack of dawn, to catch the train to London from the sticks. Big jolt of caffeine in a sandwich bar near the tube, then I walked down Great Portland Street to Western House, where the studios are.

My very first offering for the *Breakfast Show*, in June 2010, didn't mention prison specifically, but it certainly had those experiences at its foundation. I spoke about exam season and how I still had anxiety dreams about A levels all those years later. Life often seems about being put to the test, I mused, but what marks us out is how we react when the testing times come. It's interesting that religious people will often say that "God has put them to the test". I don't believe that every difficult, sad, or bad thing that comes our way is necessarily from God, but I do believe that in some mysterious way, whatever *does* get chucked at us, God's in the mix somehow.

Often that presence of the divine might be like the quietest whisper or the gentlest touch – a reminder that however we deal with our situation, we're not alone.

Chris was lovely to me that first, rather testing, time – in fact he's lovely all the time, and hugely encouraging. He's a real gentleman, who always stands up when I come into the studio and greets me with a hug. My first impression on meeting him was that he's a lot taller than he appears on TV and a lot more handsome. It's quite an education watching him as he does his stuff. It may all come across as zany and haphazard, but the man's astonishingly professional, an incredibly quick thinker, and in possession of boundless energy. To see him announcing the next record, whilst scanning a list of guests, listening to his producer and tapping something into the computer, puts my multi-tasking efforts on the *Daily Service* firmly into the shade. But when it comes to the PFT slot, he gives it his full attention. He really does listen, and off air we touch on some profound stuff. I'd love to spend a few hours over a pint or two with him, but it hasn't happened yet.

The main body of the Pause is written in advance and sent to the "strand producer". When I first started that was a producer from the BBC, but now the slot has been outsourced to an independent media company, TBI (The Big Idea), and the producer is employed by them. The allocated time is only about 90 seconds – it's quite a skill to come up with something topical and meaningful for such a small window, especially in the middle of such a fast-paced show. One senior producer I know has called it the "hardest slot on radio". After a style and delivery based discussion with the producer, the script is checked by someone senior for accuracy and appropriateness (compliance) and it is finally cleared for broadcast the afternoon before the day of transmission. It's still possible it might need to be changed, if there's a notable news event or the death of a significant person. For example, at one stage we were all asked to submit a potential script for compliance, to be stored in case we were the presenter on the day of Nelson Mandela's death. But usually the script is then fixed and it's not acceptable to change it in any material way without further compliance – a lot of trust is put in us, I think.

However, it's not as simple as reading a pre-agreed script, as anyone listening to the show will be able to tell. For a start, it's no good if the script sounds read – it has to come across as spontaneous and conversational. And in any case, this *is* live radio, with a master of the unexpected. Chris will always have a chat with you before going on air, during the song playing before the PFT slot. Often the minute or so of unscripted conversation that comes next, on air, is an extension of that chat, but you never know which way he's going to take it, and you have to be ready for anything. He's even asked me if I wear kinky boots! (Occasionally, I replied…) This can get you into all sorts of trouble though. One Christmas he and I were messing about during the song, and he came out with a naughty joke about a Christmas tree, which I had heard before but which still got us giggling. The faders went up, we were on, and, eyebrows raised, he asked me the provocative question from the joke, about my Christmas tree: "Did you put it up yourself?" On automatic pilot, and before I could stop my mouth opening and the words tumbling forth, I heard myself coming out with the punchline (look away now): "No, I put it up in the living room."

There was a split second of stunned silence from us both. His face was a picture, the studio team fell about in the tech room behind the glass, and I plunged straight into my *Pause for Thought*, all the while thinking, "Oh my goodness, I'm done for with the BBC *and* the bishop now!" Off air again, and I apologized profusely. Chris shook his head, laughing his socks off. No one complained and I think I earned my spurs that day.

The Breakfast Show broadcasts from the sixth floor (I always take the stairs) and there's a green room to wait in until the appointed time. Over the years I've sat in that green room with all kinds of people – Peter Shilton, Frank Cottrell-Boyce, Richard Hammond, Brian May. I don't usually wear my dog collar to Radio 2, so it can come as quite a shock to the other guests when they find out I'm a priest. I've had a few complimentary (but very un-PC) comments!

This is where the Glamvicar tag came to the fore. The reaction I received in the early days of the *Breakfast Show* appearances echoed comments made throughout my church career: "You're *far* too glamorous/sexy/attractive to be a vicar." That's a dreadful, and inaccurate, stereotype, but in some ways I can't help smiling to myself. Good. Every step of the way I've wanted to challenge the view that a person of faith is de facto cheesy or disconnected from the real world. And I get hugely frustrated by the assumption that because I call myself a Christian, I must therefore be a sour-faced fundamentalist determined to take society back to the Dark Ages. Nothing could be further from the truth. I have no trouble holding evolution and God in the same world view; I don't hate gay people; I agree that too many horrific things have been done in the name of religion. And as far as entertainment is concerned, I feel strongly that one can enjoy fashion, music, raucous comedy or whatever, and believe in God at the same time. Whilst there are limits – usually of good taste – there's no need to be a killjoy, and even a bit of religious satire is a good thing. One time I was in the studio when Chris's guest for the day was John Cleese. When Mr Cleese found out I was a vicar, he was distinctly cool towards me – probably because of the hard time the Python team had over the film *Life of Brian*. Sadly I didn't get the chance to tell him I thought it was hysterical.

Anyway, soon after I started on the *Breakfast Show* I joined Twitter, and needed a "handle". Glam Vicar seemed the obvious choice, as it summed up the two sides of my life and personality perfectly (although I have been criticized by one retired clergyman for calling myself a "vicar" as technically this is a parish-based title. Puh-lease). I play up to the handle a bit now – in a competitive world it's good to have something that helps people remember who you are. It's not that I'm after celebrity (a poisoned chalice, I suspect), but I do think that the PFT slot is a brilliant opportunity to put spirituality into the public arena – how else do you get a pulpit of millions? I hope I'm good at it, and I'd like to carry on.

Not everyone is of the same positive opinion though. I have had very unpleasant comments directed at me, either on Twitter or through the email facility of my website. Usually it's from religious types, along pretty misogynistic lines, and often the haters can't cope with the dual nature of my public persona – priest and entertainer. I've been told I should decide whether I'm a celebrity or a true servant of God, been called a false prophet, and even declared a "disgusting whore". But this only strengthens my view that there's both a need and a place for people like me and that religious fundamentalists of any stripe should be challenged at every opportunity. Putting one's head above the parapet is bound to attract the trolls and brickbats but I try to be part of an intelligent public discussion about religion and spirituality in today's world.

Although my two parallel careers might seem worlds apart, in fact they have a lot in common. Both call me to face down stereotypes, dealing with the nuts and bolts of life from a spiritual angle without (I hope) being too cringeworthy, taking the religious conversation way outside of the boundaries of the church, into pubs, hairdressers, cross-channel ferries... and prisons. At the same time as just being me – the woman who likes to paint her nails and dress up, who finds caring for her appearance to be an act of self-love after a rough ride, but who's also more than familiar with the cold winds of life on the edge.

It can be hard juggling the two strands of my work – heading up a chaplaincy team is a more than full-time job and I'll often end the day totally spent. It is not the best recipe for going home and creating an amusing and engaging radio programme. And there is the ever-present need to be sensible about what I put into the public ear – security, security, security. I do have a great relationship with the National Offender Management Service (NOMS) press office though, and they are very supportive of what I do. Even so, I sometimes find it difficult to balance the calling of a priest to speak truth to power and at the same time stay within the boundaries imposed on me as a civil servant. There have been government decisions and policies I have vehemently disagreed with, and keeping one's personal integrity intact whilst also keeping one's job can be a conundrum.

Not many prisoners listen to Radio 2 or 4, it has to be said. But some do, and they're thrilled when they recognize my voice. "Can't you give us a shout out, Miss?" they ask when I'm walking about on the wings. Still, they're more likely to be listening to National Prison Radio. This is a fantastic initiative, which started in Feltham Young

Offenders' Institute in 1994 as a local project, but which is now a national digital station, broadcasting 24 hours a day into prisoners' cells via the in-cell TVs. The content is made by prisoners, exclusively for prisoners, and provides entertainment, education, and support. It's won awards, and by involving prisoners all over the country in making programmes, the station teaches vital employment skills too. Unfortunately I've never worked in a prison which has had the resources, staff, or willingness to get involved in making programmes for NPR, but I have recorded several slots for broadcast, and I'm always encouraging prisoners I work with to listen in.

I probably have more inroads with the prison staff through my radio appearances – plenty of them do listen, and again, I think they're quite proud of me as a colleague, because I'm showing a different side to what they do. There's growing interest these days in prisons, (which makes a change from indifference) but so often there seems to be a tendency to concentrate on the failure of the system, and the only time prison staff are considered is when there's an officer who steps the wrong way over the line. Don't get me wrong, I'm fully aware of the shortcomings – far too many men and women in jail, dwindling resources, overcrowding, and continuing recidivism. I worked with some staff whose behaviour was really inappropriate, and totally at odds with the standards you would expect. They were dealt with by the Governor when it came to light. There were not many, but it only takes a few to give the rest an undeserved bad name. This is why, when I can, I take the opportunity to talk on air about some of the realities of working in jail, including the hugely positive work that goes on – demystifying the world behind the walls and combining my two roles.

One way I can do this is during Prisons Week. Every year a wide group of Christian organizations sponsors this national getting-the-issues-out-there event. Traditionally, Prisons Sunday has been marked in churches on the third Sunday of November, and since 1975 Prisons Week has followed on in the week after (although it's changing to a different week from 2016). The idea behind Prisons Week has been to raise awareness of those affected by imprisonment – the prisoners, of course, but also their victims, the families of offenders and victims, the prison staff, and those involved in the wider machinery of justice. It's essentially a Christian event, although I have argued for some years that, as a vehicle for discussing the impact of faith and hope in a dark environment, it should be widened out to include those of other faiths and none.

Still, Prisons Week is a great opportunity for widening awareness of the human impact of imprisonment. One year I recorded a series of audio vignettes for BBC Three Counties Radio (my local station). I interviewed a Crown Court judge, a prison governor, a victim of crime, a former prisoner and the girlfriend of a prisoner, and then distilled the interviews down into 2-minute slots, each of which aired on separate days over the week. The common factor in all of them was the vital importance of belief in change, and support from wider society. "Coming to prison might be the first time they've ever met a positive role model," said prison governor Ian, about the men in his charge. "There's sometimes a school of thought that prisons are just warehouses. We're not; we can't be. We've got to be in the business of changing people, and assisting people to change their lives."

In 2012 I led a Radio 4 broadcast on Prisons Sunday, from the parish church for the prison, St Peter de Merton in

Bedford. As well as the "live" prayers, hymns, and sermon, we had pre-recorded some prayers and songs with serving prisoners, and these were played as part of the broadcast. A line from one of the songs, specially written by a prisoner, and quoted here with his permission was:

"I am not the same, everything has changed… I changed my life within a prison."

I hope that my radio appearances, as well as being huge fun, can show the world that change *does* happen for some people, and the hope that faith engenders can be part of it.

CHAPTER 9

CARROT OR STICK?

The media's played a particular, and generally positive, role in my life, but it's usually a different kettle of fish for someone inside. If a person has committed a particularly heinous crime, you can be sure their face is all over the papers and the internet. I've not done jury service yet – the first time I was called up I was within the ten-year exemption period for having been a lawyer, and the second time I was nursing a small baby. But it must be very difficult to consider facts in a case which has been splashed all over the news. It's hard enough when you encounter someone as a chaplain, already knowing what it is that someone's done. Generally I try not to find out first – I'll be informed if there is a particular risk, or circumstances that I must know about, otherwise I try to meet the person cold. It's a matter of prison etiquette that you don't ask someone what he's done – you wait until the information is offered. But sometimes you can't avoid finding out the crime – it's been on the news, or even, once, I knew the man personally. I must remain professionally detached, remembering I'm not there to be judge and jury – that's already happened. Neither am I there as commentator. That's already happened (a lot) too. I'm there to treat this person with humanity and try to help them find a constructive way forward.

Still, I'll never forget the first time I came face to face with a high-profile offender. I was an assistant chaplain at a High Security men's prison, and it was my turn to do the stats: fulfilling the legally required (statutory) duty of visiting newly admitted prisoners, those on the hospital wing, and those held in segregation.

After a quick chat with the officers on duty, I unlocked the gate to the seg, and walked down the corridor, looking into the cells through the observation hatches that were placed at eye level in the cell doors. "How are you today?" I'd ask. "Anything you want to chat about?" Sometimes they wanted a phone call or to complain about some protocol or other. They might ask to go on the list for Sunday services or request a visit from the imam. Occasionally I'd open the hatch on a troubled, depressed man, who desperately wanted to hear some words of comfort or hope, and then, with the door open, and a prison officer on hand, we'd talk for a while, maybe pray.

When I got to the last cell on the right I was expecting more of the same. I opened the hatch and was taken aback to see the face of someone whom I felt I knew. I didn't, of course, but his face had been so prevalent in the media, and comments about his offence so widespread, that sitting-rooms across the nation must have considered him as familiar as a minor celebrity.

But here, in the slightly dingy light of a well-used cell on the block (as it used to be known), his notoriety gave him nothing. The monster portrayed and vilified by the press had long fled, as the reality of both the present and the likely future had begun to sink into this young man's mind.

We didn't talk for long on that occasion, although we would in forthcoming weeks. But I went home that evening with the realization that, for most people, this prisoner would remain simply a two-dimensional image, a collection of words and impressions gained from the papers and the internet. Whatever we in the Prison Service might come to discover about him, whatever we might do in our attempts to redirect his trajectory in life, in fact his long-term future on the out would remain largely determined by public perception of his crimes.

Crime, and its fitting punishment, has long occupied the words of social commentators, the pens of fiction writers, and the minds of late-night TV watchers. I'll admit to being a bit of a crime drama addict myself, and I've noticed that the fictional representation of wrongdoing tends to follow the same division as opinions on real misdemeanours. On the one hand there's the fairly straightforward police procedural. The villain's usually an out-and-out baddie, cleverly evading capture; but only for so long, as the forces of good finally triumph and cart him (usually him) off to the custody suite (think *Taggart*, or *Poirot*). Then there's the more complex psychological drama (the Danish hit *The Killing*, say, or the BBC's probation drama *Public Enemies*) where everyone ends up with a faint whiff of culpability and the end leaves a lingering degree of uncertainty.

While the UK was freshly reeling after the summer riots in 2011, this same dichotomy could be seen in public and media comment. The rioters were either nasty little morons who should be banged-up and the key thrown away, or they were poor little darlings who'd never had a chance and all they needed was love and understanding. That's perhaps a rather sarcastic parody of the extremes, so here are two of the comments actually made at the time:

> Combine understandable suspicion of and resentment towards the police based on experience and memory with high poverty and large unemployment and the reasons why people are taking to the streets become clear [...] Those condemning the events of the past couple of nights in north London and elsewhere would do well to take a step back and consider the bigger picture: a country in which the richest 10% are now 100 times better off than the poorest, where consumerism predicated on personal debt has been pushed for years as the solution to a faltering economy, and where, according to the OECD, social mobility is worse than any other developed country.
>
> **Nina Power,** *The Guardian,* **8 August 2011**

> An underclass has existed throughout history, which once endured appalling privation. Its spasmodic outbreaks of violence, especially in the early 19th century, frightened the ruling classes.
>
> Its frustrations and passions were kept at bay by force and draconian legal sanctions, foremost among them capital punishment and transportation to the colonies.
>
> Today, those at the bottom of society behave no better than their forebears, but the welfare state has relieved them from hunger and real want.

> When social surveys speak of "deprivation"
> and "poverty", this is entirely relative. Meanwhile,
> sanctions for wrongdoing have largely vanished.
> **Max Hastings,** *Daily Mail,* **10 August 2011**

I met a few of the youngsters charged, and later convicted, as a result of those calamitous summer nights. My prison, like others up and down the country, had to gear up for the extra numbers coming through our gate, as magistrates sat through the night to hear their cases. It was up to my team to interview the newcomers in the first 24 hours and try to establish some sort of rapport with them, find out a bit about their background. Some of those sent to us lived up to the stereotype: aggressive, confrontational. But far more had shocked themselves, and couldn't explain what had possessed them. Finding themselves in jail for maybe the first time ever, they weren't sure how to respond to their circumstances.

I'm not sure society has worked out what it wants those circumstances to be. The punishment versus rehabilitation debate continues, with the balance shifting according to the political zeitgeist and the prevailing financial climate. The Prison Service states that its aims are to "protect the public and reduce re-offending", but that can be interpreted in a number of different ways. A strong deterrent, some would argue, fulfils that purpose as much as a more constructive regime.

They have a point – to a certain degree. I've met a few, particularly those on very short sentences, who quite literally see their sentence as a brief retreat. I vividly remember one man smirking at me and telling me the judge had given him the choice of either carrying out community service or coming to jail for three weeks. He'd opted for jail, despite its privations, because he could spend the time sitting around not doing much – he saw it as a holiday. And if that's your attitude, a sentence of a matter of weeks probably is a bit of a lie-down, if you can shut your eyes and ears to the surroundings. There just isn't the time to process someone and get them into meaningful work and education, let alone do any rehabilitative work with them. Commentators far more learned than me repeatedly question the value of such short sentences and I hope that the unfolding changes in policy, probation, and community supervision address that.

But what *does* constitute a deterrent? Greater brutality? A bread and water diet? Hard labour? Long sentences for everyone? Apart from the serious question this raises about what kind of society we are, some men are so brutalized, so used to a walled-in existence, that prison, no matter how tough the regime, isn't much different – in fact it's more of what they've come to expect from life in general. I've found that the real breakthrough often comes when a man is confronted with an attitude or an experience he *didn't* expect.

I've generally had a good relationship with the Independent Monitoring Board in the prisons where I've worked. The IMB exists to provide a non-affiliated ear and voice to those in jail: holding the authorities to account, receiving complaints from prisoners – taking action where appropriate, observing practice and procedure. The members are volunteers, often giving many hours of their time, and usually possessing an earnest desire to see positive outcomes for prisoners. One morning, ploughing through the usual umpteen emails, I saw one from the Chair of the IMB.

"My wife," the email read, "is a fellow of a Cambridge college. There's a group of students at the college who have formed a choir – they're very keen to come and sing to, and more importantly with, prisoners. Interested?"

You bet.

I met with Joe, the choirmaster, over a cup of coffee. He was a former student, passionate, theatrical, inspired by the idea of bringing music and beauty to a group of people not usually considered in the world of arts. He headed up an outfit called CaMEO: Cambridge Music Educational Outreach. They had worked with kids in the past, but contact with a criminology PhD student had sowed the seed of working with prisoners.

So the plan was hatched and four months later I met seventeen wide-eyed students at the gate. Each one of them had to be security checked to come into the jail and they'd received an email from me outlining the dos and don'ts – bring photo ID, no mobile phones (that was a shock), don't talk about your personal lives. As they arrived I made a mental note to tell the next lot (if they came again) that the girls should wear trousers or long skirts – these young ladies were going to cause a stir...

You wouldn't believe the amount of work that goes into organizing an event like this. All the visitors must be cleared, which involves obtaining full name, date of birth, place of birth and occupation, before sending off for a check on the Police National Computer and collating the response. Visitors need to be instructed about prison rules – summed up neatly as "Nothing in, nothing out." In other words, you may not bring in any items other than those permitted for personal use (and check what they are), and you may not take anything extra away with you – no letters, no messages, no packets of cigarettes.

It's a serious one, this. An unsuspecting visitor could be duped – "Miss, you look lovely. Thanks for coming in to see us, you're a great person, so different from the rest of them in here. Look, it's my daughter's birthday next week, and the post here takes ages, I really don't want to miss her special day, it'd mean the world to me just to get a card to her. Could you just pop this in the postbox for me on your way home?"

It appears to be the most reasonable request in the world. Except this prisoner is banned from contact with his daughter because he raped her. His outgoing post is usually checked for addressee by prison staff, so he's circumventing the safety net. Imagine the feelings of his victim to receive a card from him in the post on her birthday…

So visitors coming in have to be briefed. They all need their ID checked on arrival and they wear ID badges. I need to make sure I clock how many visitors there are, who they are, and what they look like. It's not going to be very likely to lose a girl (although I still have to make sure one doesn't literally get lost, or dragged off somewhere), but the guys are a different matter. Some male visitors I have in (even some chaplains!) dress in such a way that they don't look much different to the prisoners – I don't want one of them to go wandering and end up banged up in a cell by mistake, or for a prisoner to disguise himself as a visitor and walk out with the group at the end of the day. For this reason I've had to tell some of my chaplains to smarten up their dress code – not only for professional reasons, but so they can be more easily identified.

Visitors are one side of the coin. Organizing the prisoners to take part in an activity is another. Everything in jail is governed by a list. If your name is not on the list, you don't attend the event. Except it's never that simple. For a start, my current prison is in a local jail – which means it holds remand and short-sentenced prisoners mainly from the local area. The upshot of this is that the turnover, or churn, of prisoners is significant, up to about 5,000 men in and out during the course of a year. Because of this, lists can only be compiled a few days in advance – otherwise most of your signatories will have moved on or out. Furthermore, space and numbers are limited – risk assessments and staffing levels determine how many can attend a particular event. If your list is over-subscribed, you have to decide who can come and who can't. I might be a chaplain but playing God like that doesn't make me popular!

Once the list is compiled, then the names have to be checked by security for suitability. Then you might have to negotiate with other activities (education, gym, work) to obtain permission for Mr X to attend your event. And you hope on the day that the wing staff get the correct list, and unlock the correct prisoners, on time. And that the signed-up prisoners don't change their minds...

Once the prisoners do finally arrive (amidst all the arguments about who has been allowed to attend and who hasn't) they must be searched at the door of the venue (usually the chapel), always by hand and sometimes with a dog too. This is to try to weed out (excuse the pun) those who are using the occasion to deal drugs.

Then during the event I must keep an eye on behaviour, answer left-field questions, police the scrum for the biscuits and squash, watch the visitors to make sure they're sticking to the rules and not getting freaked out, answer the phone, listen to my personal radio for instructions from the control room, and watch the clock so the prisoners are back in their cells when they should be.

Of course this always goes smoothly, all of the time. Ahem.

There are days when I think enviously of my parish colleagues and wonder how they'd feel if their church events were like this. And that's before we get to Sundays when I'm also supposed to lead a service, say prayers and deliver a semi-coherent sermon! I'm sure it's why I have developed quite a caffeine habit (gin not allowed in jail...) – although I suppose it should really be chamomile or something equally soothing.

On this particular day we surmounted all of these obstacles and brought together seventeen earnest Cambridge students and twelve rather wary prisoners. They stood in a circle, and Joe began leading them all through some voice exercises. I know from singing lessons I once took that doing these feels really silly – and before long the men were giggling like kids over their "Me me me meeeees" and "Mah mah mah maaaaaaahs".

One of them was Liam – a right little so and so. He was always in and out of jail, with his cheeky-chappy persona and his mess of a life. Drugs – small-time dealing, big-time taking, anytime theft, sometime violence. He'd assaulted prison officers, fought with other inmates, given us the run-around in chapel services. Goodness knows how we'd managed to persuade security to let him come – but we did, arguing it was lads like him who needed the intensive rehabilitation work more than the good boys who knuckled down and did their time quietly.

But we, and he, knew he was on thin ice – if he messed up today he could kiss goodbye to any more chapel activities.

That morning the choir taught and rehearsed the men in four songs, using simple harmonies and catchy tunes. They took them from giggling kids to men who were surprised at the sound they could make. The plan was that in the afternoon they'd re-convene and deliver a short concert to other prisoners.

The men were sent back to the wings for their midday meal and the lunchtime bang-up – an hour and a half of being locked in their cells. Meanwhile the staff had a full staff meeting with the governor, at which the choir were due to make a presentation about their work.

Staff meetings are held on a monthly basis in the chapel as it's the biggest available space. All the uniformed staff troop in from the wings, while the civvy staff emerge from the offices, classrooms, and clinics. It's a chance for the governor (or deputy) to deliver information, admonishment, team-building, or whatever, and for some cross-pollination from departments. With such large numbers of uniforms present, it's usually an intimidating gathering, particularly faced with the habitual cynicism of the men and women in those uniforms. How would they react to the news of a choir disrupting the usual regime, I wondered?

Joe stood up and began to talk about the potentially rehabilitative effects of getting men to sing together; effects such as team work, listening to others, improved self-esteem, presentation skills, and even the uplifting effect on mood that comes from music. I could see a few raised eyebrows. What made those eyebrows shoot to the heavens was Joe's next line.

"Right!" he said from the podium. "To prove my point, now we're all going to sing." And with that he unrolled a large sheet of paper, on which were the words of the Beatles' song *Let it Be*.

I cast a glance at the Deputy Governor (Dep) who'd gone pale. On the other side of him was our good value Head of Security – I could see she was up for it. Joe launched in, and about half the staff gradually joined him. At which point he abruptly stopped, strode down the aisle to the back, stood amongst the white shirts and said, "Come on, you lot – you have an example to set when you're back out on the wings – let's see you all singing!"

Never in my life did I imagine I'd see those burly prison officers singing at work – let alone mostly enjoying it – but they did. Afterwards some were laughing and clapping each other on the back, others were muttering curses – but they'd never forget the day music came to the prison.

Neither would the prisoners. The group came back that afternoon and gave a fantastic performance to their peers. It was incredibly moving to see these men, most of whom had achieved very little in their lives, singing harmonies with some of the most elite students in the world. Liam behaved perfectly, and he even teamed up with another prisoner, who was getting over a recent bereavement, to encourage and support him. It wasn't just the prisoners who gained something, though. The students, so nervous at the start, had their preconceptions challenged, and their eyes opened. Prison has the potential to change everyone, not just the inmates.

The choir came in on several occasions after that and each time Liam attended. His behaviour improved, he began to demonstrate respect and self-restraint. Some months later we held a week-long Building Community event throughout the jail, with the choir and other community visitors coming in. There were competitions for prisoners and projects like decorating on the wings to enhance the environment. At the end of the week we presented certificates to prisoners who had distinguished themselves. Liam was one of them. He came to receive his certificate in front of his peers (always an invitation to bravado) and a handful of senior staff as well as wing staff.

Once the applause died down, he asked to speak. "I'm known for trouble," he said, "and I'm not exactly the screws' favourite" (cue sniggers and grim nods, depending on status), "but I've achieved something and it all started with the choir. They believed in me, and showed me I could do something I didn't think I could. I'll never forget singing with them, even though they're posh. We were all the same and I never expected that."

One of the governors spoke to me afterwards, shaking his head and smiling. He couldn't believe it was the same Liam that he'd had to discipline on so many occasions and he was deeply impressed with the possibilities he'd seen unfold through the music.

There are sections of the media who would disagree vehemently with these kinds of programmes – seeing them as privileges that prisoners should not have. But I believe the arts are not just a nice extra or a luxury in *anyone's* life – music, art, theatre, poetry, and literature are as essential to our humanity and our progress as engineering and science. Perhaps this is precisely because they are *not* task-focused and utilitarian, instead taking each of us on a journey into our own heart, and thereby helping us travel a little into the heart of someone else.

I received a letter from another prisoner after that first choir visit and concert. He was an older man, had suffered with depression whilst inside, and tended to keep himself to himself. In some ways what he wrote was incredibly sad but it also showed the impact that day had. "I really enjoyed singing with the choir," Terry wrote, "and being with the other prisoners, who I didn't know. The young people who came in were so good to give their time and made us feel relaxed. I've never sung before, but I would say now that it was the best day of my life. Thank you."

Unexpected positive experiences can stop a man in his tracks and help him to re-evaluate the narrative of his world view, rather than have him repeat the same knee-jerk responses to rejection and negativity. But it's not just emotions and pre-conceptions that can be affected. It's well known that prisoner literacy and educational levels are poor. It might not be immediately obvious that chaplains can have any input into tackling this but in fact we can: by bringing these arts-based events into the jail. Through the media of music, art, and drama we can teach history, ethics, language. We can raise awareness of social issues, world events, the lives of others. We can encourage mutual respect, teamwork, perseverance.

One year the Lantern Theatre Group came to Bedford to perform a play about the life of Corrie ten Boom. Miss ten Boom was Dutch, a practising Christian, and lived with her family in Haarlem. During the Second World War she and her family hid Jews from the Nazis, and were incarcerated in concentration camps for their pains, her sister eventually dying in one. The men who came to watch the play were spellbound. These were lads who usually can't sit still for thirty seconds without yakking, let along an hour and a half in complete silence. And at the end, amongst the appreciative comments and the obvious learning that had gone on, one young Irish traveller lad came up to me. "Do they do that sort of thing on the outside, Miss?" he asked me. I told him that all kinds of people did plays about all kinds of things, and if he enjoyed it, he could always go to see something else one day. "I will, Miss," he replied, "I will. It was great. I never thought that kind of thing was for the likes of me."

I so hope society can make sure it is for the likes of him, and the likes of anybody who is so inclined, because sometimes in this way is salvation found. I wish we could open up our collective minds and hearts, as well as those of these men (and women, of course, although after the girls in the youth facility, I haven't worked with female prisoners).

I think back to those times in my life when I was made to feel stupid, when I felt rejected and worthless. Did they make me a better person? Most definitely not. They made me a more angry, confused, sad, insecure person. And that anger, confusion, insecurity, and sadness leached out into my life, where it wreaked havoc on my mental health, my relationships, my working life. Does treating a dog harshly make it a better dog? More obedient, sure. Out of fear, not respect, and certainly not love. And given half a chance, that fearful dog will bite.

FACE TO FACE

It was a Sunday morning and the recently appointed bishop had come into jail to lead the morning service. Apart from a brief greeting at the recent formal ceremony to welcome him to the diocese I'd had no contact with the chap and no idea what he was like. But that morning I knew I had to tell him something he wouldn't want to hear. This could affect my career all over again. Sitting in the office after the service, cup of coffee in hand, I waited for the volunteers to disappear. Once we were left alone, the bishop and I chatted about the men that morning, the work in jail, and how he was settling in. OK. It was now or never.

"Um…" I began, in a small voice. "There was something else I wanted to speak to you about, bishop." I wondered if he might actually be able to see the pounding of my heart through my black vicar shirt. "The thing is, unfortunately, my husband and I have split up and I will be moving out shortly."

Gulp.

"I guessed as much," the bishop replied, surprisingly gently. "You're not wearing a wedding ring. Come and see me later this week."

After more than a decade of doing my best I had come to the end of the road. Living in separate bits of the house was agony for us both and the children had begun to notice. Years of unhappiness take their toll and, despite our efforts, what had always been a difficult relationship had become unbearable. For the whole family. I realized this was a dreadful failure, against all I tried to live by, but I had to leave. I knew some people would castigate me – even without knowing any of the details (they did). But I also knew family and true friends would understand (yep, right again). I could see it would be a hard road ahead, even if I was able to keep my job (being a chaplain still requires the bishop's licence, and they tend to take a dim view of one divorce, let alone two). I would have to move out, leaving behind the lovely home I'd created. I'd have to house myself (no vicarage when you're a prison chaplain). The children would have a bomb put under their lives. His parish would be affected (although I had played very little part there for years; as it happened, many hardly noticed).

I had a small amount of savings, painstakingly built up over about twenty years, and a life insurance policy to cash in – together it was a four-figure sum, not loads, but enough for a 5% deposit in the government's Help to Buy scheme. I hesitated for weeks before finally signing on the dotted line – which meant that I would become the owner of a tiny little new build, not yet complete, on a nearby development. I finished work one July day, signed the contract at the estate office, and went back to the vicarage shaking inside. I fed the children fish fingers, gave them a bath, read the story, the whole bedtime routine, tucked them in, and walked downstairs. This was the moment I had agonized about, stepped back from, prayed about, cried over for years. All my hopes and dreams, rescued and rebuilt from the pit of depression, were shattered in pieces on the floor: again, after all those years. And I was no longer young – I was in my mid-40s, with two school-aged kids and two just out of adolescence. Could I do this? I didn't hate my husband. If I'm honest, I'd had times when I did (and it was probably mutual), but I was way beyond that now. If anything, I didn't want him to waste any more of his precious years either – he's fifteen years older than me.

How the most important times in our lives are reduced to clichés. "We need to talk," I said. And talk we did. Talked, and then sat in stunned silence for a bit. We cried a little. He didn't disagree, didn't protest. I could see he was grateful I'd taken the step he hadn't felt able to.

I remember him saying, "You're right. Thank you. You've been very brave." I told him I'd bought a house, that I would move out, that I wouldn't air our dirty linen. And then I went out – and walked and walked, for miles, in the dark. I felt so very guilty – I knew we'd both failed in so many ways – but I was also deeply relieved. I knew in my heart that I was doing the right thing and somehow it would be OK.

Those next few weeks were a flurry of packing and solicitors' letters. We explained what was happening to the kids. Bright little sprogs, they'd already worked it out. We came to an agreement over how they'd keep a strong relationship with us both. We sorted the money side of things. We tried to be fair. The release of tension in the house was palpable. Now that we were no longer trying to be husband and wife we could be (almost) friends, and help each other through these traumatic few weeks. When I finally moved in to my little terrace, he even came and put up the curtain poles for me.

We've continued to be civilized and supportive (mostly) ever since. When he discovered he had cancer a couple of years later it was me who drove him to the hospital appointments, who waited for him during the five hours in theatre, and kept in touch with his family when he could not. It was such a contrast to the agony and hostility when my first marriage imploded. We were different people of course: older, wiser. But maybe it's also a symptom of a relationship that died long before the final chapter – much of the conflict and hurt had happened years before.

That's not to say it was easy after I left. After the initial relief, I grieved. I couldn't work out whether I was grieving for the relationship or the loss of my home and my hopes. It was probably a bit of both. I doubted my decision several times, questioned my actions. Because so many of my family and friends viewed the end of this unhappy marriage as a good thing I couldn't share my feelings of sadness with them. I kept my promise not to air our dirty linen, but of course, my clergy colleagues could then only see calm, friendly, generous behaviour between us. This confused them, I think. Judging by the reaction of one or two, I was confirmed as a scarlet woman, leaving behind a marriage that didn't look so bad from the outside.

The new bishop was great. He wanted to know why, of course, and questioned me thoroughly. I may be tucked away behind prison walls, but I'm still representing the church – and I'm doing it via the media too. So my behaviour had to be scrutinized. Of course there are many in the church who see divorce as a dreadful sin, and some who feel I should not be a priest. But, thankfully, there are others who see individual situations more deeply than that – my bishop being one of them. I would keep my licence as a priest – and my job.

How ironic that at a time when I was rebuilding my personal freedom I should be working with men behind bars. And how fitting, at a time when I was feeling so broken and such a failure. Face to face with my own shortcomings, not only in recent times, but over decades, I finally saw the real me. It wasn't a shock-horror revelation, because I found compassion for the damaged young person I had once been, and admiration for the obstacles I had overcome. But still, the sweep of the years lay before me, the bad decisions, the half-recoveries, the self-deception. I saw the folly that led me into that second, ill-fated marriage. I saw the immaturity and struggle and feelings of rejection that marred the first. I revisited the battles with authority figures, and realized I'd been longing for approval all my life. Even my pain at being excluded from church life cut more deeply because the church was my substitute parent. And all of this had hurt others as well as me. It was time to grow up. To approve of myself and not seek approval elsewhere. To care for myself, not long for others to do it for me. To live by myself and not fear being alone.

Owning our story can be hard but not nearly as difficult as spending our lives running from it. Embracing our vulnerabilities is risky but not nearly as dangerous as giving up on love and belonging and joy—the experiences that make us the most vulnerable. Only when we are brave enough to explore the darkness will we discover the infinite power of our light.

Dr Brené Brown, research professor at the University of Houston Graduate College of Social Work

We can get so caught in the turmoil of our lives that sometimes it takes something dramatic to lift our gaze to the bigger picture. The vast majority of my charges in jail have never stopped to think about their reasons why. They've never really reflected, in that brutally honest way, on their decisions and choices and the impact they've had on others. Restorative Justice aims to encourage just that by bringing offenders face to face with their victims, or if not the person they hurt, then at least someone who has been on the receiving end somehow.

Prison chaplaincies have been involved with this idea for a number of years, often, but not exclusively, through a course called Sycamore Tree, which is run by volunteers from the Christian organization Prison Fellowship. The title of the course derives from the symbolism of the sycamore tree in the Bible – supposedly meaning eternity, divinity, and strength. It also references the biblical story of Zaccheus, a much hated tax-collector, who climbed a sycamore tree to spot Jesus from afar. Much against social convention, and to the disgust of onlookers, Jesus called Zaccheus down from the tree and promptly invited himself to supper.

The Sycamore Tree course is run in prisons over a number of weeks, via the chaplaincy, with up to twenty prisoners who have opted in voluntarily. Styling itself a "victim awareness" course, a significant moment is when the participants are confronted with a genuine victim of crime. This can be the proverbial wake-up call for many, although, clearly, reoffending is a complex interplay of factors which only rarely is going to be stopped in its tracks by a single personal revelation. Nevertheless, it has its impact.

Ray and Violet Donovan are a couple in their sixties. Trained Restorative Justice facilitators, they participate regularly in Sycamore Tree courses, as well as speaking more widely in prisons and schools. Although my chaplaincy has not had sufficient funding to run a full Sycamore Tree course, Ray and Vi spoke to a roomful of prisoners at HMP Bedford in 2013. They are specifically qualified to talk about the impact of crime, as their 18-year-old son, Christopher, was murdered by a gang of teenagers in 2001.

This is how they described the dreadful event to the *Daily Mail* in 2012:

> He had been walking down a nearby street with Phil [Chris' younger brother]… A gang of nine youths attacked Phil for no reason and when Chris tried to help his brother, he was kicked to the ground as well. The gang used Chris's head as a football, throwing his unconscious body into the road where he was hit, then dragged along by a car.

Amanda Cable, *Daily Mail*, **12 September 2012**

Devastated by their loss, the couple struggled to carry on with life. They couldn't bury their son for sixteen weeks because of the need for a post-mortem and then they had to face the agony of the trial. Three of the teenagers who had attacked their sons were found guilty of murder. Two got life in prison with a minimum of nine to ten years. The youngest was detained at Her Majesty's Pleasure, to serve a minimum of six years.

But as time went by Ray and Vi realized that they couldn't carry the weight of grief and bitterness without it destroying them. Practising Christians, they resolved to forgive the boys who had taken their son's life. So they consciously let go of the anger, the human desire for revenge. Admirable enough, the story could have could have stopped there. But it didn't.

The description of what happened a few years later is taken from a piece written by "Peter", a contributor to the online blog "Thought for the Week".

> Several years later, one of the young men contacted Ray and Vi asking to meet them to say sorry. [...] In July 2011, after the young man had completed his sentence, a meeting was arranged [...] Ray and Vi hugged him and said he was forgiven. He whispered his thanks. Ray said, "My wife and I left that meeting feeling like a weight had been lifted. Just hearing the words 'I'm sorry' is a start to moving forward. For us it was a life changing event."
>
> **www.thoughtfortheweek.co.uk, 24 September 2012**

This remarkable couple take their story to prisoners across the UK, not shying away from descriptions of the raw pain they suffered and the anger they had to learn to put aside. Their purpose is to make prisoners aware of the ripple effect their crimes have, affecting people they might never have considered. They are candid about the ongoing losses – of not having grandchildren via Chris, of the empty space at Christmas. It is deeply affecting, and I remember some of my prisoners being moved to tears as they listened. When they left the chapel afterwards, there was not a word spoken, but their faces said it all.

From time to time we hear or read stories in the media of people who have forgiven the person who caused them so much grief – parents, partners, victims themselves. They refuse to let someone's actions destroy every bit of their life and they choose to move on. Often they start up charities, or campaigns, to address the issues which have affected them so deeply. These people don't always get the chance to meet the perpetrator; sometimes they don't want to, and no one should feel under pressure to do so. And of course, plenty of times the offender (in whatever context that word is used) doesn't want forgiveness, feels they have done no wrong, and therefore has no remorse and no intention of changing their behaviour.

But that doesn't neutralize the power of forgiveness in the life of the victim. I can understand those who can't forgive and would never think less of someone because they can't. Please, God, may I never have to wrestle with the murder of my child.

The Donovans have set up a charitable trust in their son's name. On the website (www.chrisdonovantrust.org) they have posted a letter written by a young man who served time in HMPYOI Feltham, and who heard them speak:

> I have wasted two years of my life in jail through bad choices and being around older people who at the time were into drugs and guns. I wanted to impress them so I decided to take a gun […] and robbed the […] people that they had trouble with through dealing drugs, at the time I was not thinking about the consequences of my actions […] I got six years ten months, I was only fifteen at the time and I never thought of the people […]

Many interventions for prisoners that started out historically being done by the chaplain – victim awareness, community resettlement, family care, counselling – have gradually made their way into the mainstream, albeit no longer faith-based. The Ministry of Justice is now very much behind the principles of Restorative Justice, but prefers direct victim–perpetrator meetings rather than more general victim awareness like Sycamore Tree. A leaflet produced by the MoJ states:

> RJ gives victims a chance to explain to offenders the real impact of their crime, to get answers to their questions, and sometimes, an apology. It gives victims a voice and the chance to play a part in preventing others from becoming a victim of crime. It can be part of repairing the damage and can help the victim to move on.
>
> RJ also provides a way for offenders to face up to their actions, understand the devastating effects their crimes have had on the victim and their family and, where possible, make amends. In this way, RJ can help stop offenders from re-offending.

The leaflet also sets out the ground rules:

> RJ is voluntary for both the victim and offender and only takes place if a trained RJ facilitator decides that it would be safe and suitable. RJ can be done in different ways. Sometimes it's right for a victim and offender to meet face-to-face, other times they can communicate by passing messages back and forth through a trained facilitator. The key thing is that it helps both the victim and the offender.

Research suggests that up to 85% of victims who participate in Restorative Justice find it a satisfactory process and there are emerging statistics to suggest a quantifiable positive impact on re-offending. But the important line for me from the Ministry of Justice leaflet is that Restorative Justice should "*help* both the victim *and the offender*". The bright light of self-knowledge is vital. Like an alcoholic or any other addict, the burglar or assaulter or drug dealer isn't going to stop without an awareness of the damage done. They need to take personal responsibility for the character flaws, the behaviours, the compulsions behind the offending. Face to face with himself (I deal with men, remember) he must look directly at the consequences of his actions, own them, and in some way make amends. This is at the heart of Restorative Justice.

But it can't stop there. For too many, the cold hard look in the mirror can be a devastating reality with no obvious way forward. Restorative Justice at its best will incorporate real restoration, so far as is possible, for the offender as well as the victim.

It's a minor comparison, but when I was standing in the ruins of yet another marriage, I faced my demons. But I needed more than that. I needed someone on side. I needed a job, so I could have a home and provide for my children. I needed someone to understand the complexities of my experience, the reasons for my actions, and the genuine nature of my sorrow. I needed friends and I needed hope for the future. That would help me walk the road towards genuine restoration.

When I took up my post at Bedford prison, in the summer of 2011, I inherited from my predecessor a place on the Board of Trustees of a charity which provided support and befriending to ex-offenders. The Community Resettlement

Support Project (CRSP) had been set up under the umbrella of the chaplaincy three years earlier, and aimed to match prisoners being released with volunteer befrienders from the community. The befriending partnership was to last for up to twelve weeks for each individual, providing personal support and signposting to community services while the newly released person found their feet. It's a pattern followed in many areas across the UK, often faith-based in origin, but operating in the community for people of all faiths and none. This community chaplaincy usually aims to be an extension of the support available via the prison chaplains, but unlike prison chaplaincy (part of the Prison Service budget), community chaplaincy is usually entirely charitably funded.

CRSP was a tiny operation in the face of huge need. Covering Bedfordshire and Hertfordshire, but with only three full-time staff and a part-time administrator, the bulk of the coalface work was done by volunteers (again). The volunteers were drawn from all walks of life – retired teachers, businesspeople, students. Together the team worked to provide that extra mile so often needed when someone's trying to make big changes. Referral to the service came via a chaplain or a mental health worker or maybe a prison officer who had discussed the individual's needs post release and felt befriending would help. Participation wasn't compulsory and prisoners needed to agree to the process. You can't help to change someone until they're ready to change – that moment of revelation needs to happen.

Most post-release services recognize that there is a "golden hour" and a "golden 24 hours" after release. In that first hour, the newly released prisoner might meet either a positive influence or a negative one. His drug dealer might be waiting round the corner, ready to pick him up and suck him back in again. Or his mates might be in the pub down the road, ready to soak him in booze once more. In the first 24 hours, he'll either make it to where he should be – home or hostel – or he'll get waylaid, waste the discharge grant (only just over forty-two pounds – hardly a fortune), and probably find himself in trouble all over again. So a CRSP worker would try to meet the newly released client as the gates opened: a friendly, familiar face, hopefully enough of a diversion from the temptations waiting just around the corner. If he needed to get to the station she'd take him there. If he had an appointment at Probation she'd go too. If possible, she'd also take him straight to meet his community volunteer and over coffee they'd discuss what his immediate needs were.

Meetings were always in public; volunteers were always trained. Despite the meticulous planning, though, it didn't always go smoothly. Sometimes the client would decline any further input or be back inside before Bob was the proverbial uncle. One was taken to a bed and breakfast room, then, as the adult he was, left to his own devices. He managed to get drunk, fall asleep, and leave the basin tap running... cue one flooded room and one very irate bed and breakfast owner.

But there were definitely some success stories too. Every year CRSP had to produce an evaluation report, to demonstrate to funders and other interested parties it was doing what it should. Here is a short extract from the 2015 report, telling the stories of two ex-offenders who made use of the service:

"M was referred to CRSP from Bedfordshire Probation Trust. His main goal was to get onto a college course for a B Tech qualification, so the Resettlement Support Worker matched him with a befriender who is currently a student at the University, in the belief that this would provide him with a helpful role model.

The befriender commented that when he first met M he didn't present himself very well; he was slouched in the chair and didn't even say hello properly. So in the weekly befriending sessions he coached M on how to present himself more positively when he meets people or even just speaks to people on the phone.

They also completed a budgeting skills exercise, and M began to try his best to keep to the budgeting plan that they worked out together.

M was very positive about his experience with CRSP; he was accepted onto the college course and felt this was down to the fact that he had a befriender to help motivate him. He felt that his befriending sessions were productive in different ways each time. He said, 'My volunteer has really helped me sort myself out. He listened to me, and I looked forward to our meetings. I sorted out a fine the other day; before I met my volunteer I would just have left that – but I rang around and chased it up and paid it off. I never would've done that before.'

B made a self-referral to CRSP after seeing our posters on the prison wing. Having been in and out of prison for a number of years he had decided that he was ready to make positive changes in his life.

With help from CRSP's Resettlement Support Worker (RSW), he set out his aims. The main focus was on gaining employment on release, and the RSW met with him several times during the weeks prior to his release. She referred him to training inside HMP Bedford where he could practise for his CSCS test [required for work in the construction industry] and apply for photo ID and a birth certificate on his release. She also referred him to NACRO [National Association for the Care and Resettlement of Offenders] who helped him open a bank account. And he attended a 'Reducing Barriers to Re-Offending Day' in HMP Bedford where voluntary organisations and employers attended from the Bedfordshire & Luton area.

B was particularly interested in gaining employment and experience in plastering and managed to impress an employer. He had continued contact with the employer prior to his release which showed his commitment. Once released B found it very difficult to stay positive in the face of temptations such as drugs, crime and old friends, but he gained emotional support and encouragement from his CRSP befriender, who helped him see that he was already making progress.

B's main aim has been achieved and he is now working for the company he met inside HMP Bedford. He said, 'the extra support from my CRSP befriender helped me to stay positive and keep focused on my goals. They helped me to help myself.'"

Sadly CRSP no longer exists – funding pressures and a changing environment for small third sector providers just got the better of us. It was an incredibly hard decision to close the charity, because we felt we were making a real difference, but we couldn't continue. The workers were made redundant, the volunteers thanked and despatched – and my chaplains and I continue to look for creative (but cheap!) ways to underpin those men who've had their moment of revelation and genuinely want to make the change. There are fabulous organizations and charities continuing this work, like the St Giles' Trust, but there's no substitute for local, on the ground intervention, from the very communities in which these men belong. One of the ways I hope to create an avenue for this is to involve local faith communities much more – churches, mosques, gurdwaras.

Strong community is hugely important, particularly for those who are trying to break away from a life of offending but in fact for us all. My support in the days after my second marriage breakdown came mostly from my colleagues within the prison. Like many crisis services – the police, military, emergency medics – prison staff stick together. Whilst there may be a fair amount of verbal jostling and even sharpness on a day-to-day basis, when a colleague's in need, either on the job or in private time, there's no hesitation. So I had help to shift my furniture on moving day, plenty of post-mortem conversations over a cup of coffee, and even the odd spot of childcare. One colleague left a lunch tin full of goodies on my desk, another baked a cake for the kids. With long-standing friends far away, and very little immediate family, those small gestures reminded me I had a place amongst a community.

It works the other way round too. If a chaplain's done their job right staff will turn to them in their own time of need, whether or not they have a faith. That can be over a personal matter – marriage problems (Ha! Am I an expert to be consulted or in fact a fellow disaster area?!), maybe debt, or a work-related issue. I've been called upon to facilitate workplace mediation, helping two members of staff resolve differences without the need for a formal grievance procedure. If an officer is assaulted, it's important one of my team checks up on their well-being. We can be a safe space to let off steam about a boss, a new policy, and the daily demands of the job. My colleagues have come to trust me, and it's a precious thing.

The strength of the prison community shows most clearly in the face of tragedy. Frank was an experienced and highly respected officer, liked by prisoners for his genuine interest in them, and loved by colleagues for his great sense of humour and commitment. A talented guitarist, an artist, and a father, he was one of those people who seemed to be living life to the full. At work one January day some of his fellow officers noticed he just wasn't looking right. One of them took him to the hospital, stayed with him while he had some tests done, then brought him home. About a month later we were shocked to hear the diagnosis. Frank had a brain tumour.

His colleagues and friends rallied round, visiting Frank and his long-term partner, Jo, and helping in any way they could. When it became clear that the tumour couldn't be cured, Frank's major concern was for Jo's future. I went to see them, and we discussed the possibility of marriage, which would be not only a poignant statement of their love, but would also secure financial security for Jo. While the prison governor worked through the internal bureaucracy, I began to explore the options for their wedding.

Initially we hoped Frank might be able to make it to his local church for the ceremony, but he deteriorated rapidly and I had to find an alternative. There is a procedure in the Church of England for marriage by Special Licence. This is granted by the Archbishop of Canterbury, and gives permission for a marriage ceremony to be conducted outside of church premises, and without many of the usual precursors like reading the banns. It's used most often for a bedside marriage in hospital, when one of the parties is not expected to recover. We needed to get this wedding organized pronto, so I contacted the Church of England's legal office, and they sent me the relevant forms by email – thank goodness for modern technology.

Over the phone later that day the legal adviser discussed the case with me and said he didn't see there would be any problem in the circumstances. It was a pretty straightforward procedure as long as neither of the parties were divorced or a foreign national.

Oh.

Frank was divorced and Jo was a US citizen with the right to remain in the UK.

More forms ensued, to be submitted with a report from me as to why this marriage needed to be by special licence, alongside photocopies of passports, official documents, doctor's letters. It was a whirlwind of paperwork, phone calls, and delicate pastoral conversations. We got there in the end, within a week. The day was set and the archbishop sent a letter of support to Frank and Jo.

It was one of the hardest things I've ever had to do as priest. I married them in their sitting room, with just his parents in attendance. As ill as Frank was, he made himself stand for the entire ceremony, and despite difficulties with speaking, he said those vows with all his heart.

Only a matter of weeks later, Frank passed away. Where I had once been the priest who married him, now I had to conduct his funeral. That was the day when I witnessed for the first time the extent of the prison community. The prisoners all expressed their sorrow and respect, offering words of condolence to the men and women locking them up. Officers and governors from other jails came to take over duties for the day so everyone who wanted to could attend the funeral. And at the crematorium, amidst the several hundred mourners, prison officers in "No 1" uniform lined both sides of the road to the small chapel, as the hearse proceeded slowly between them. Straight-backed, grim-faced, upholding each other, they were united in grief and duty. I felt as if I had a huge responsibility, not only to Frank and his family, but to these men and women, his colleagues and friends, who needed to be led in a dignified way. I hope I achieved it – I think I did – and I was incredibly moved to be part of that "professional family" on that day.

Prisoner, minister, officer – we all have failures, sorrows, and vulnerabilities. Face to face and side by side, we can use them to grow.

LAND AHOY

"So how about this sailing malarkey then?"

Those seven words were to change my life. Richard was a Regional Chaplain, a kind of area overseer, and together with the governor, had interviewed me for my post at Bedford Prison in 2011. Our paths had crossed sporadically afterwards and we got along well but no more than that. He was a keen sailor and frequently invited colleagues, friends, and acquaintances to go out on his yacht to try the experience. He'd asked me once, and I'd thanked him, but decided not to follow it up. I knew my husband and kids would not have enjoyed it and as a married woman it didn't seem quite right going alone, even though there was clearly no ulterior motive on his part.

But in the months after I set up home on my own I was keen to expand my horizons, as well as develop a social life to sustain me in the times the children were away with their father. I met up with girlfriends I hadn't seen for ages, hosted supper parties, and accepted invitations. Scrolling through my phone contacts list one evening, I realized I still had Richard's mobile number. "Why not?" I shrugged, and sent the fateful text.

He didn't seem bowled over at the suggestion but we fixed a date and he sent me an intimidating list of dos and don'ts, along with suggestions of what to wear – something warm, flat shoes, nothing precious. Durrr. I would have thought that was obvious. But as he later told me, "Not at all." He'd had people turn up in heels, little dresses, thin clothing. I suppose they'd imagined it would be very St Tropez, when in fact the sailing yacht, *Fantastic Feeling* was a 29-footer, very much designed for sport rather than G&Ts on the top deck. And she was moored in East Anglia, not the South of France...

Thankfully, I got it right, and was well-festooned with jumpers when I arrived at the sailing club on the River Orwell. I needed them, it was bloomin' freezing! The yacht was on a mooring out in the middle of the river, so we pootled out to it, balanced precariously in a little rubber dinghy, which was powered by a grumbling outboard motor. The surprisingly clear, but somewhat chilly water was only inches away, and I began to wonder what I had let myself in for. As we pulled up alongside the yacht I clocked that there was no ladder. The sides towered above me. So exactly *how* am I going to get on board? Seconds later I was wobbling on the edge of the dinghy with Richard's hand firmly planted on my derrière, as I hauled myself up and over the stanchions. Very dignified.

After a barrage of instructions about what to do if he fell overboard, most of which I promptly forgot, Richard fired up the yacht's engine, dropped the rope tying us to the mooring buoy, and we set off down the river. All fine, until he looked at me and said, "You take over the steering now." Now I love driving. Put me behind the wheel of a car (preferably sleek, low-slung, and fast) and I'm a happy woman. But this was a nearly ten-metre-long boat. With a tiller. And with a tiller you have to move it in the opposite direction to the one in which you wish to travel. Heck.

By the end of that chilly day on the water I had learned how to steer in a straight line, how to tie several different knots, and how the wind acts on a sail. I was hooked. There was the exhilaration of feeling the boat leap under your hand when the sails fill, a perfect harmony of nature and human skill. The weak sunlight sparkling on the gun-metal grey water, the brittle calling of curlews across the mud-flats, even a seal poking its whiskers above the surface to eye-ball us as we glided by. As we slipped through the tide, back towards the marina and the mooring, I knew I'd have to do this again. And not just because of the sailing. Somewhere deep down I felt something shift in the fabric of my life – did he feel it too?

When he kissed me, standing in the galley, after yet another warming cup of tea, I knew he did.

I've often thought that one of the things missing from the lives of those in prison is beauty. In truth, for many, it's probably been missing for much of their lives. Prisoners have pictures of their girlfriends on the walls, often fairly startling photos it has to be said. They think their women are beautiful, and their children, and rightly so. But there's a wider encounter to be had: the experiences of standing in a field at dawn as the mist clears from the valley below; climbing a mountain and taking in the breath-taking panorama; listening to Mozart or Elgar and being moved by the sweetness of the music; or standing at the water's edge and breathing in the freshness and vitality of the sea. Through poverty, lack of opportunity, and a middle-class stranglehold on the arts and travel, beauty is denied to many.

That's why arts programmes like the Cambridge choir, theatre groups, and even faith festivals are so important inside. We are less than human without colour and soul. Prisoners often listen to violent, raw-sounding music – little wonder, it mirrors the condition of their own spirit: alienated, angry, bitter, combative. Yet when given the opportunity to paint, write, play music, what emerges over time are often works of extraordinary gentleness and care. I've seen painstaking models made out of matchsticks – sure, when you have all the time in the world, anything to while away the hours keeps you sane – but men create castles, roses, sailing ships. I knew a man who made the most intricate origami models – his forte was a swan, with a gracefully arched neck and ruffled feathers. And I frequently receive poetry, usually about faith, as men try to articulate their reaching for something better, something more. This is a poem, called "Rosary Rap", written by a Catholic prisoner, Glen, about how he held on to the prayer traditions of his religion:

Why is there a pain
But no release
An it all never leave
I honestly believe
Coz there's a pain inside
That lies beneath
And when I say beneath
I mean underneath…
An there's hardly
Any air an it's hard to breathe
An it's all pure pain
But no release…
An I get upset

And emotionally…
So I pray sometimes
With my Rosary…
So hopefully
God grows to me…
An maybe one day
Looks over me
I can feel him lookin down
Lookin over me
And he's telling me be GOOD
And there's HOPE for ME…

It's that magic word again – hope.

My current prison is a grey, stone and brick place, with only functional outside areas. On a drizzly January day, it must be one of the most depressing places in the country. There is not much beauty to be seen there. But in a previous jail where I worked, a group of prisoners, under the tutelage of a talented horticulturalist, created a stunning garden and wildlife habitat which has since won an award in the national Wildlife and Gardens Closed Prisons category. With a pond, wooden seats, and distinct areas representing different types of garden (desert, alpine, grasses, and so on), the garden is a focal point at the very heart of the prison. Whilst it was being carved out of the bare soil, I'd often stop to talk to the men in the gardening party on my way from one wing to another. They were learning skills which would make them more employable upon release, often gaining qualifications as they dug and sculpted and planted. But possibly even more importantly than that, they were full of pride at what they were achieving, as well as bursting with childish excitement when the resident moorhen had chicks, or a particularly difficult plant bloomed successfully. The garden was a powerful symbol of beauty and possibility, right in the middle of an institution containing society's greatest "no-hopers".

Of course there will always be those who remain impervious to any attempt to uncover their soul, men so far mired in the mud of their deeds and delusions that reaching them has to be left to the Almighty alone. But I firmly believe that we don't encourage someone to be a decent human being by dehumanizing them. Better to focus their gaze on what they could be, what life could offer, in contrast to their diet of quick fixes, fleeting highs, and endless, empty brutality.

Sonny came to the confirmation classes I offered to chapel regulars. He had a bad reputation and was often in trouble for fighting on the wings. He was a drug-dealer and carried on his behaviour in prison. One brother in a large family, most of whom were in jail, he reacted to the smallest slight with foul language and his fist. Wing staff kept him on a tight rein, for obvious reasons. When he signed up for the classes the security department raised a collective eyebrow. It was to be a small group, so there was less scope for misbehaviour, but I knew I'd have to keep an eye on Sonny. I wondered what his motivation was, too.

In fact, as I looked round the rag tag bunch who'd turned up for the first lesson, several of whom had issues with each other, I questioned briefly whether I'd get anywhere with this crazy plan. The idea was to take a small group of prisoners, regular attenders at chapel services, who had been christened as babies, and lead them through a course designed to prepare them to confirm the baptismal promises as adults. They had signed up voluntarily, and committed themselves to three two-hour sessions. At the end of the course we would hold a special service on a Sunday morning, inviting the bishop in to perform the ceremony of confirmation.

We looked at journeys that first session. Physical ones, places they'd been, but also emotional and spiritual journeys – where they'd come from and where they'd like to go. They each had a chance to speak if they wanted to, to tell their story and express their hopes. Sonny shuffled uncomfortably when his turn came but after a stuttering start he began to speak about the harshness of his upbringing and the violence that was seen as his initiation into adult life. As a young boy he was encouraged to settle disputes with his fists and he was beaten when he cried. His family moved from pillar to post so he always felt like an outsider. He didn't learn to read and achieved little at school. Ridiculed by his peers, always in trouble, he fell back upon his family, turning inwards and pulling up the drawbridge. Petty crime turned into drug-dealing, providing money more readily than low-grade employment ever could. Sonny had never learned to control his deep-seated anger and it erupted in violent outbursts, particularly against anyone who challenged him.

"But there's something different now," Sonny continued. "My little boy. I don't want him to have the kind of life I did. I don't want him to grow up angry, and end up like me. I've come to church because I don't know where else to go. This is the only hope I have left. I want my life to be different, but every time I try I screw it up." And then he turned to one of the other men sitting in the group, a resident on the same wing as Sonny.

"One of the things I know I have to do," he said, looking down at his feet, then back up into Martin's face, "is to say sorry to you, bro. I know I had a go at you on the wing, and I shouldn't of [sic]." Reaching out his hand to Martin, I could see Sonny gulp. He'd made himself incredibly vulnerable. We all held our breath. Martin's face crumpled into a grin and he reached for Sonny, pulling him into a hug.

As the classes progressed, I assigned each participant a role in the forthcoming confirmation service. Two were to read from the Bible; two would write and say prayers. And I asked Sonny to say a few words about why he'd chosen to get confirmed and what he hoped for the future. This was a big ask – speaking in front of your peers is no easy thing and the presence of the bishop in resplendent robes would only make it more intimidating. On the day, Sonny spoke briefly, awkwardly, but the shaking in his voice still couldn't disguise his newfound dignity. His peers applauded him loudly. Sonny had found a way to be something more than the sum of his disastrous past.

Sonny still has anger issues and still gets into trouble. Once I was standing with him by the pool table while he was visibly seething with anger and inches away from grabbing the pool cue to lump someone with it. Out of the corner of my eye I could see the officers inching in, and I knew I'd have to make a swift exit if it turned nasty. In a low voice I spoke to him soothingly, as one might to a distressed child or a nervous pony. "It's all right Sonny," I murmured. "Remember your little boy. Remember the bishop, that service, all that you hope for. Get through this." It won't be an easy journey for Sonny, but he's glimpsed what he could be, and I fervently hope and pray that's the light that will lead him safely to shore.

Sometimes it's something far less dramatic that makes all the difference and reminds a prisoner of his humanity. It could be the simple act of a handshake, in a place where no one touches, unless it's in anger or to impose restraint. It might be the keeping of a promise, or a smile, in a place where trust is fragile and eye contact can mean trouble. It might be reminding him that whatever the world at large might think of him, you know the journey he's been on, and you respect the efforts he's making.

As my relationship with Richard grew my family were delighted. My ex was unfazed, he himself establishing his own new relationship. However, I began to be concerned about the world at large for myself. One colleague had told me some months before that "because of my context" (i.e. another divorce), fellow clergy "would find it hard to respect me". Since the end of my second marriage, I'd battled to re-establish my integrity as a person and as a priest. In truth I'd been fighting for that for the best part of my ministry. I hadn't shared publicly the vast majority of the struggles of previous years, nor would I, but the cost of this was my being cast in a dubious light. But I was slowly winning the fight, I thought. I'd begun to open up a window on a mysterious world, and my colleagues had started to see the value of what I did. My bishop had been very supportive after the marriage break-up. How would these people take the news that I was involved, seriously, with someone else?

A bit like the recent case involving the hospital chaplain, Jeremy Pemberton, if the church authorities deemed my lifestyle or actions to be incompatible with my role as a priest, I could have my licence revoked. Although I'm employed by the Prison Service, not the Church of England, it's a requirement of the job that I'm in "good standing" with my ecclesiastical authorities. In other words: no licence, no job. Now I had done nothing illegal, nor had I, in my view, done anything immoral (no adultery, for example). But I was still worried that if Richard and I were to wish to marry that could be a problem. Even I can see that three marriages isn't exactly ideal. I realized I could be faced with the real possibility of having to choose between Richard and my lifelong vocation.

So we hesitated for a long time. But in that time I learned to sail, fulfilled a lifelong ambition to visit Australia, climbed the big three UK mountains, and wrote an entire suite of Christmas carols with a composer friend, which were premiered at St Martin in the Fields. My creativity, energy, and inner joy soared. Of course this was a side effect of being in love, but I also had a sense of finally travelling in the right direction. I had learned to live alone, which meant being with someone else was a choice, not a compulsion. I tried to embody forgiveness in my everyday work, which meant I had learned to forgive those who'd hurt me, and, more importantly, myself. I had confronted my demons and my failures, which gave me strength for the future pilgrimage. A friend had said to me, "Don't build your own walls around yourself, and don't let others build them either." I had finally trudged my way to inner freedom and was a better person for it.

So, in the end, after seeking the advice of trusted friends, and perhaps rather unromantically, we made the decision to marry and take the consequences. Our families were delighted. Ever the social networker, I took a deep breath and posted the news on Facebook… Wow! The messages of love and support were breath-taking.

And my fears about the censure of the authorities proved unfounded. The big cheeses were lovely. The wedding plans commenced.

Fears and concerns aside, I was free to make a decision to marry and then just get on with the plans. Prisoners have the right to marry in jail and, of course, since the changes to marriage law in the UK they have a right to marry a partner of either sex. But they still need to ask for permission. Occasionally I've received applications from men seeking that permission – but it's not up to me; it's in the gift of the governor.

There's a set procedure, which starts with the chaplain talking to the prisoner about the marriage plans, and then, if it looks promising, meeting the couple together during an official visit. I need to discuss the future with them – do they understand the implications, especially the non-imprisoned partner – and particularly if the prisoner's inside for a lengthy stretch. Then there are the public protection issues – checking the partner's not a witness, or a victim, and is aware of the full offending history. Are there children? If so, what are the implications for them or issues surrounding them? They need to have enough money for the registrar's fees too. My thoughts and recommendations will go to the governor, along with the prisoner's application. It is unlikely the governor will give permission if the prisoner is within three months of the end of his sentence, unless there are pressing personal circumstances, such as serious illness or the impending birth of a child. The governor will also take into account any information that I don't have access to around security issues and so on.

Many of the governors I've worked with have been of the opinion that if a wedding can reasonably be avoided in jail, then so much the better. Not for their own convenience, and not to deny someone their civil rights, but because it's not exactly an ideal place for such a significant occasion. But if the prisoner is eligible, and there are no legitimate reasons against the marriage taking place, then permission will be granted. Some lower-category prisoners might even be given permission to attend an outside venue for their wedding.

When a wedding takes place in jail there can only be a very small number of guests, all of whom have to be security checked. The ceremony is likely to take place in the visits hall, in front of a registrar. Chaplains *can* conduct a ceremony in the chapel, but a registrar needs to perform a legal ceremony first, away from religious premises, unless it's a Church of England wedding, where the priest acts as registrar as well. And of course, many religious bodies do not allow their representatives to perform same sex marriages, whatever the views of the individual minister, so again, this would need to be overseen by the registrar. As far as a celebration goes, it might be possible for a cake to be ordered in, or even made, by the kitchen (not brought in by the wedding party), but there's not going to be a full-on reception. No champagne. Limited photos. No wedding night or honeymoon. If the prisoner is on the escape list then he may have to attend his wedding in the characteristic, brightly-coloured harlequin clothing assigned to men at risk of absconding.

A marriage is far more than a wedding day though so if the couple can cope with the limitations, and the marriage is going to bring stability, then good luck to them. It can be a vivid symbol of hope and redemption, to exchange promises in a place usually associated with the more dismal things of life. And getting married can be the turning point that helps a prisoner finish his time and rebuild his life.

Richard and I decided we wanted our sailing history to form the basis of our wedding day and so we settled on a ceremony on board HMS Warrior, a magnificent Victorian warship permanently berthed in the Royal Naval Dockyard in Portsmouth. For two priests used to conducting religious weddings we found ourselves on unfamiliar territory as we negotiated the requirements of a civil ceremony, which was all that was allowed on the ship. We wanted a family friend to perform a service of blessing immediately after the legal bit, as seamlessly as possible, so we had to negotiate a way for the registrar to scurry off the ship pronto. This was because she had to have her feet on dry land before the religious aspect could begin. Meanwhile the priest friend needed to dive off to a side room on the ship to don his robes once the registrar left, as he wasn't allowed to wear them while she was present. What a palaver!

As with all weddings, there were large chunks of the day that were perfect and a few bits that turned out to be slightly less so. It poured with rain, the photographer was unfriendly and bossy, and the caterers dropped my gluten-free pudding on the way from the kitchen. But the wedding team on the ship made it a fantastic occasion. We were surrounded by people who'd stayed the distance with us, we walked out of the ceremony to the strains of Captain Pugwash and gales of laughter, and my elder daughter described the day as "The best pirate wedding ever" (an accolade indeed from her!).

As the evening wore on, my quiet, shy, elder son stood up to give a speech, something I knew he was terrified of but had been determined to do. With a catch in his voice (and tears running down my cheeks!) he told the room how glad he was for us, having known the challenge of the journey. "I can see this is the happiest day of your life, Mum," he said, "but let me say it's also one of the happiest in mine, too. I'm so proud of you, after all you've been through, and I'm so pleased to be here with you both today." Our friends roared their approval.

Richard and I left the ship around eleven, with the party still going strong. Our hotel was close by and we had planned to walk back alone. It was pouring with rain, but the harbour lights twinkled brightly against the blackness of the water lapping close by. We stepped carefully down the slippery gangway, picking our way through the puddles, and onto the quiet streets.

As I remember that scene now, and the deep calm I felt as I stepped from ship to shore, the words of one of my favourite hymns come to mind:

"Lead us, heavenly Father, lead us, o'er the world's tempestuous sea;
Guard us, guide us, keep us, feed us, for we have no help but thee:
Yet possessing every blessing, if our God our Father be.

Saviour breathe forgiveness o'er us; all our weakness Thou dost know.
Thou didst tread this earth before us, Thou didst feel its keenest woe.
Lone and dreary, faint and weary, through the desert Thou didst go.

Sprit of our God descending, fill our hearts with heavenly joy;
Love with every passion blending, pleasure that can never cloy.
Thus provided, pardoned, guided, nothing can our peace destroy."

HEARTS TO HOLD

When my first child was born, twenty-five years ago, the snow lay thick on the ground outside. I'd had a difficult labour – the baby was a breech presentation and although the delivery was natural it had taken place in theatre ("just in case") with what felt like scores of people looking on. We were taken up to the ward in the middle of the night, my daughter and I, wheeled silently between rows of beds, the occasional glow of a bedside lamp or the urgent mewling of a newborn piercing the hush and the dark. The windows in our bay were ill-fitting, so the sub-zero temperature leaked inside, setting up a draught that curled around the edge of my cubicle curtains. I knew I wouldn't sleep, so I lifted my tiny girl into the bed and laid her close to my exhausted body. She spent her first night on earth nestled in the crook of my arm and the fiercest love was born.

Like any new parent I felt the weight of responsibility wrap around me. By the morning I had learned that this precious life was in my hands, and every action, every word, would have a weight in the years to come.

I've been privileged to hold another three children in my arms, to see all four grow strong and curious, uniquely themselves. I've also seen them bear some of the burden of my own mistakes, my own all-too-human imperfection. But they have always carried love with them, and, I hope, a belief that the world can be a kind place, at least in part. I have tried to impart to them the sense that they can both receive of, and contribute to, that kindness.

We're all given hearts to hold. For some of us it's those of our children. For others it's those of partners, parents, friends. Many of us manage, in our clumsy way, to keep those hearts safe and warm, even as the cold winds blow.

As a priest in prison, I've been given even more hearts to hold – ones that have hardened and blackened, and thumped with anger and hatred and fear. When lives are left untended, bruised, and abandoned, it takes a mighty effort to undo the harm. It takes an investment of years, an unflinching determination, and a willingness to pick up the fragile pieces again and again and again. I know that the men I deal with have caused untold damage, to themselves and others. I know they've broken the hearts of their parents, their children, and those they preyed upon. I hear the pain of victims, the anger of society, and I'm glad I don't bear the burden of administering justice.

During my time as a chaplain, I've got to know many who do bear that burden. I've been greatly impressed by the seriousness and humanity with which the judges approach their duty. They can be deeply compassionate, and although there's a fair bit of black humour amongst them, they can also be moved by some of the more pathetic cases that come before them. They try to see the individual standing before them, reaching for decisions to help instead of hinder, avoiding prison unless it really is the only option. As Judge Foster said to me once, "If in doubt, keep 'em out." They sometimes agonize over a judgment and, like all of us in the field, there are cases that will haunt them for ever.

Getting to know the judges has provided a third side to a triangle in my career, giving it a kind of completeness. I've been a solicitor shrinking under a judge's stare. I've spent years with those on the receiving end of sentences. And now I've had the chance to see the men and women under the wigs.

That glimpse of the other side of the coin has been reinforced by my appointment as the Chaplain to the High Sheriff of Bedfordshire for 2015–16. The office of High Sheriff goes back about a thousand years and the incumbent was originally the king's representative in the county for law and order. The High Sheriff would ride around making sure folk paid their taxes and didn't rustle the sheep. These days it's a largely ceremonial role, albeit still a royal appointment, and the High Sheriff usually champions good causes connected to the justice system. In another throwback, the chaplain officially becomes part of the Sheriff's household for the year of tenure (although thankfully there's no obligation to take up residence in the spare bedroom…). It's the chaplain's job to provide support and counsel to the High Sheriff as he or she (it's been a she during my year) goes about official duties.

There is an annual Justice Service in each county, usually held at the senior church in the county and attended by the region's judges. The focus is to pray for the justice system and the administrators of the law. It's full of pomp and circumstance. There's much be-robed processing on the street, holding back the traffic and providing wonderfully anachronistic photo opportunities for the local press. The service is usually followed by a reception and during my year of being Shrieval Chaplain it amounted to dinner in a beautifully refurbished manor-house-cum-wedding-venue a few miles from Bedford.

I'd been given the task of saying grace but with the proviso that it was a funny one. I scoured the internet for ages, but most of them were either naff or only suitable for a room full of servicemen. I went to bed one night shortly before the dinner with the task very much on my mind. Inspiration struck about midnight and I leapt out of bed to write down the ditty I composed, sure it would have flown away by the morning.

At the appointed time on the evening I rose and made a pre-emptive apology to the guests from the police for the use of the vernacular:

"Whether lawyer, or justice or plod,
Councillor, cleric, M'Lud,
Whether saint or a sinner,
It's time for our dinner,
So let's thank the Lord for our 'fud'."

The company roared, although I saw the bishop wince slightly – living up to my reputation again! We sat down to eat, an earl and countess, several eminent judges, assorted High Sheriffs, a Chief Constable (who forgave me the plod), the bishop, and various other dignitaries great and small. Glam indeed. But how crazy that I was here, in the middle of all this! What a pilgrimage for an ordinary woman with a colourful story, somehow straddling the gap between the highest and lowest in society. And as we ate and drank, as I listened and enquired, the gap grew narrower and narrower. It's surprising what people will reveal to a priest, even after just a brief meeting. We all have our dark corners and our tender places, our narrow squeaks and our shameful episodes. Some overcome them by birth or wealth, others by fortitude or chance. Many more don't manage it at all – swallowed up by the gaping maw of poverty, whether of resources, opportunity, empathy or imagination.

In a prison system inhabited by 85,000 shapes of grey, I try, amongst many others, to bring the colours of dawn – a gradual returning of the light, instead of the unrelenting dark. Because I've met with individuals, not stereotypes. I've reflected on real lives, not concepts. And I have concluded that there are very few without a glimmer of hope. We all hold within us the capacity for right and wrong and even a monster was once a babe in someone's arms. I'm not arguing for leniency or release for those who should remain inside. I'm not championing the cruel, or feckless and selfish, as if personal responsibility didn't matter. I'm not denying the revulsion we feel at many crimes. But I am standing up for the principle that inside each heart there lies the capacity for something good, however small, and inside many of those hearts there lies the potential for transformation.

I don't know if I shall remain a prison chaplain for the rest of my working life – possibly not: there's a good few years left to go, and I'm always keen for a new challenge. But my goodness, what a ride it's been so far. I've been challenged and frustrated, meeting some amazing people and some decidedly frightening ones. I've worked with hearts of gold and heartless backstabbers, with the arrogant and the wise. Whilst mixing with the great and the good, I've also been sent to the margins of society. A bit of a reject myself, I've learned some of the most central lessons of life: courage, compassion, and a hefty dose of humour.

I've found my own healing in prison and been able to make sense of some of the saddest times in my story. And the lessons I've learned have crossed over into my more public presence, informing my words, however short a time slot they may occupy. The broadcasting work has opened up a different world for me, allowing my creativity to find an outlet beyond the bars and high walls. It's kept me going on many occasions when the pressure's been too much. It's brought me friends as well as mad frolics, and on occasion I like to think it's brought comfort, even inspiration, to the listeners. I certainly hope it will continue for many more years and I'll hang onto that "glam" image for as long as I can.

In these, my reflections on the journey so far, I've stayed away from theology mostly, so perhaps I can be forgiven one small foray. In his book *Wishful Thinking: A Theological ABC* the American theologian, Fredrick Buechner wrote, "The place to which God calls you is the place where your deep gladness and the world's deep hunger meet."

My deep gladness lies in offering the hurting heart – the searching, wounded, wondering heart – a touch of hope. I'll happily offer it through the airwaves, or on the wings, through words or by waiting in silence. Certainly through my own story. Judging by the evidence, I think there's a fair few hungry for that hope.

POSTSCRIPT

I told you God had a sense of humour. Just weeks after completing the manuscript of this book I was appointed to a parish post. It seems my years in prison have, after all, rehabilitated me. They've enriched me too. I may no longer be a prison chaplain – but I will carry with me for ever the memories and experiences my stretch inside has afforded me.

ACKNOWLEDGMENTS

Although I'd often dreamed about writing a book, it's still a delightful surprise that I've actually managed to do so. Dad, you always told me I should and here it is at last! Thank you for always believing in me and for being my friend and great example.

There are plenty of people mentioned in this book – their stories have challenged and enriched my life, and I'm grateful for the moments when our paths have intertwined, however painfully or briefly. Those whom I have hurt or let down – I'm sorry. Those whom I have tried to encourage – hold onto hope.

I have the Establishment to thank, too – the Church of England, for letting me stay, even though I'm a maverick; the BBC, for giving me airtime; the Law, for teaching me foundational skills; the Prison Service, for allowing me time to write this book, and for the career I've forged inside.

I'm so glad Lion Hudson decided to give my writing a chance – thanks, Ali Hull, for your quiet encouragement and advice, and for responding to my Facebook messages even when you were on holiday!

I probably owe an apology to my children for using them in yet another creative project – they tolerate being quoted on national radio at regular intervals; I hope their appearance in this book reminds them of how very proud I am of them and the profound love I feel for each of them.

And to Richard – my sailor. Thank you for being my anchor.

MY YEAR WITH A HORSE

Feeling the fear but doing it anyway

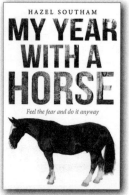

"A moving and lovely book, this isn't just about the relationship between humans and horses — it's actually about the most important relationship we have in our life, our relationship with ourselves. I know nothing about horses, but I enjoyed reading this honest and open account, a charming story."

Revd Kate Bottley, Gogglebox vicar

Hazel Southam had been scared of horses since childhood, but a huge carthorse called Duke was about to change her life for the better.

As a successful journalist, Hazel had been used to fear — reporting on areas recovering from war, famine, disease, and poverty. Then devastation struck closer to home. Her father's dementia grew worse and the strain of looking after him caused her mother to have a stroke. In the middle of settling her father into a home, Hazel caught a fever in Africa and the resulting disease threatened not only her health, but also her livelihood.

To get through the hardest year of her life, Hazel turned to a horse called Duke. Gradually, to her surprise, riding him through the Hampshire countryside became an unexpected source of comfort and solace. This is the heartwarming story of that year.

ISBN: 978-0-7459-6849-0 I e-ISBN: 978-0-7459-6850-6

wwww.lionhudson.com